CREATING LIFE
- THE PODCAST
TRANSCRIPTS

THE ART OF WORLD BUILDING

VOLUME IV

RANDY ELLEFSON

Evermore Press
GAITHERSBURG, MARYLAND

Evermore Press, LLC
Gaithersburg, Maryland
www.evermorepress.org

Creating Life – The Podcast Transcripts / Randy Ellefson. -- 1st ed.
ISBN 978-1-946995-13-1 (Amazon paperback)
ISBN 978-1-946995-18-6 (IngramSpark paperback)
ISBN 978-1-946995-14-8 (IngramSpark hardcover)

CONTENTS

ACKNOWLEDGEMENTS

Cover design by Deranged Doctor Design

FOREWORD

This collection of transcripts from *The Art of World Building Podcast* is based on a series of non-fiction books, *The Art of World Building*. That series is divided into three volumes. The first is *Creating Life*. With the exception of the Episode 22 transcript here, each episode is based on a chapter (or part of one) from that book, with additional information and tips not found there. This collection is therefore longer than *Creating Life*.

These transcripts are designed for the podcast listeners (and anyone else who wants them) to have a written copy of the episodes to take with them anywhere and not need an internet connection. They are casual in presentation and unedited, except that each episode features section breaks with music and voiceovers; the latter have been removed from these transcripts and placed in the appendix to avoid repetition.

INTRODUCTION TO THE PODCAST

Hello and welcome *to The Art of World Building* podcast, episode number one. Today's topic is an overview of the podcast and what you can expect. This podcast is based on my three-volume series of books *called The Art of World Building.* While I won't be reading from the text, I'll be covering portions of the same material. And I'll also be introducing myself and my world building experience.

Do you want practical advice on how to build better worlds faster and have more fun doing it? *The Art of World Building* book series, website, blog, and podcast will make your worlds beat the competition. This is your host, Randy Ellefson, and I have 30 years of world building advice, tips, and tricks to share. Follow along now at artofworldbuilding.com.

OVERVIEW

What I'd like to begin with is an overview of the podcast and what we're going to be covering during the episodes. For the most part, we are going to be following along with the three-volume series I have written called *The Art of World Building*. The first volume is called *Creating Life*. The second volume is *Creating Places*. And the third volume is *Cultures and Beyond*; that's basically a catchall for everything that didn't fit into the first two volumes.

I'm not going to be reading passages from the book. If you want to hear that, there's going to be an audiobook of them forthcoming, but I will be more or less following along with the content of the three volumes, starting with *Creating Life*. So let's talk a little bit about what is in each volume, so you know where we're going with all this.

THE VOLUMES

Volume 1 talks about why we should build a world or even if we need to. And then it goes on to talking about how to create gods, species and races, world figures like heroes and villains, monsters, plants, animals, and finally undead.

The second volume is called Creating *Places*, and it talks about how to create a planet, continents, land features like forests, mountains, swamps, and it's got a big chapter on understanding sovereign powers. This is something that's often not covered. In many cases, it seems like people just present everything as a generic kingdom and don't go into details of what's going on with this government and how it functions, and what the effect is on people. There's quite a bit of research I did and I basically shortened it and made it something that's easier to digest, and has a focus on what a world builder would need to know to create believable sovereign powers, and a better variety of powers.

After that, we talk about how to create a sovereign power, then how to create a settlement. And then another subject that doesn't seem to get covered much, which is travel by land, which in a medieval society or a fantasy setting, it's usually going to be horses or wagons or even mythical creatures like dragons. So how do we figure out how long it would actually takes anyone to get from one place to another unless we have a reliable way of doing this?

There's a similar chapter on travel by sea. This is a subject that most of us, unless we're into sailing, we have no idea how long it takes to get from one place to another on a boat or ship. There's quite a bit of information about that, including on ship types in that chapter. There's another about travel in space using fictional technologies.

And then we go on to talking about creating time and history, and places of interest such as supernatural phenomenon located somewhere. And then there's a bonus chapter on how to draw maps.

For volume 3, *Cultures and Beyond*, we'll talk about cultures and things like greetings, how to create a language, religions, military groups, supernatural and a system of magic, and of course magic items, and technology if you're doing sci-fi. And then there's a big chapter on how to create names and there's another chapter about keeping everything in perspective so that you don't get overwhelmed with the act of building worlds.

The three volumes don't need to be read in order, nor do their contents, and this podcast can also be listened to out of order. However, I will say that there will probably be times when I don't finish a subject in one podcast and will resume it in the next, but I'll make sure that the description of the podcast makes it very easy for you to understand when this is happening.

HOW TO START

One of the subjects that tends to trip up world builders is how to start, or where to start, so throughout the book series and in this podcast, I provide tips on exactly what to do. These usually come at the end of a chapter and it will come at the end of the podcast as well. The reason being that I think it's important to understand the subject that you're going to create before you get an idea of where to start.

So for example with gods, you need to know all of the things that you need to consider about this and figure out which ones are most important to you. Based on what I have explained, at the end I will say, "Okay if you want to do this or that, here's what you should start with. Otherwise, start on this. And here are the things that can wait until later."

THE WEBSITE

There is more help that you can find on the website, artofworldbuilding.com. Note that it is not theartofworldbuilding.com even though that's the name of the book. The website is just artofworldbuilding.com.

One of the resources you will find on that website is free templates that you can download and use while you are creating worlds. For example, each volume covers various subjects and as a result there are several templates that go with it. Volume 1, *Creating Life*, there are templates for creating a god, a species, a world figure, a monster, a plant, and animal, and an undead. These are all free to download.

There is one catch, however. You just need to join the newsletter for *The Art of World Building*. I have a separate newsletter for just that. If you are interested in my fiction, feel free to read something. You can actually read a book of mine called *The Ever Fiend (Talon Stormbringer)* for free by joining the fiction newsletter. Both of these are located on the same sign-up form so, as you are joining the newsletter for *The Art of World Building*, so that you will be emailed the free templates, you can also check another box for the fiction newsletter and you will get a link to download the e-book of *The Ever Fiend*. The link for this newsletter is at artofworldbuilding.com/newsletter.

And what are you going to get in the newsletter? Well, in addition to the templates that you can download, you're also going to get, I think at this point it's bimonthly, tips on how to do world building. These tips are drawn partly from the actual volumes. Sometimes I find other useful things out there on the Internet and I will summarize these or send you links. No one likes spam so I'm not going to send you a lot of stuff. I just don't have the time honestly to do it and you don't have time to read it if it's not useful.

ABOUT ME

So let's talk just a little bit about me. After all, you're listening to my podcast. Why should you follow my advice? Who am I? What have I done?

Well, I have been doing world building for almost 30 years now. Much of my work has been on a single planet called Llurien. It even has its own website now (Llurien.com) as I'm beginning to publish my stories and I wanted another place for people to go and find out more information. This is partly so that I'm not tempted to just go on and on about my world building and all my creations in the context of a story. We'll talk more later about this problem, which is called the problem with exposition. This website is one way of going around that.

The point I'm making is that I'm pretty much kind of nuts to have spent three decades building the same planet. I'm something of an expert. I've done just about everything that is in this podcast and series of books, so I have practical experience with everything.

Now in addition to building Llurien, I have sometimes built other worlds for just a single project like a short story or a one-off book that is not going to take place in that setting. So I've done everything from this incredibly intense and in-depth creating of one setting, and I've also done this kind of admittedly skimpy approach to just one setting that I need for one story, and I don't want to spend an incredible amount of time and detail doing that if I'm only going to use it once. And I've got some advice for you in this series about when to do what and how to decide how much to do for each of your projects.

PIERS ANTHONY ENDORSEMENT

If that's not enough to convince you that I know what I'm doing, you can take the word of best-selling author Piers Anthony. I was lucky enough to get him to take a read through of volume 1, *Creating Life*, and he had this to say: "It is exhaustive, well-written, and knowledgeable. I, as a successful science fiction and fantasy writer, have generated many worlds, so this material is familiar, but it would have been easier and probably better had I had a reference like this. It is realistic, recognizing that the average writer may not have the patience to work out all of the details before getting into the action."

For those of you not familiar with Piers Anthony, I first came across his Incarnations of Immortality series. He's probably most known for his Xanth Series, which has almost 30 books. It actually probably has more than that. I recommend checking out his work. It's pretty good!

One of the things I talk about in this podcast and in the series of books is that we need to find a balance explaining our world to the audience and maintaining our story or narrative flow. We don't want to stop our story to say "Hey here's the thing I created!" and go on and on for paragraph after paragraph about it. So I try to keep the world building practical and accessible for the audience and I think this is something that you as a world builder also need to focus on. I've got quite a bit of tips coming your way for how to do that.

As for my actual writing, I do have this three-volume series of nonfiction books. I have also written over a dozen short stories, and I've written about six novels, some of which I'm in the process of starting to publish now.

My focus is for the most part on fantasy, so much of my advice is admittedly a little bit weighted towards fantasy, but in my experience, most of it really does apply to science fiction as well. It is something like travel in space that is obviously much more of a sci-fi thing than fantasy.

As a final note, I'm also a musician. My degree is technically classical guitar but I was always more of a rocker. I have released three albums of my own instrumental rock, including the title song that you heard at the beginning of this podcast. I've also released an album of classical guitar, and one album of acoustic guitar instrumentals. So I've had a lot of experience putting together major projects and releasing them to the public and now I'm doing the same with my fiction career, and this podcast is part of that.

And last but not least, I am still a working stiff like you probably are, so I work as a professional software developer in the Washington DC area and I have my own consulting company that I've been doing for quite a while now. It's a good way to pay the bills and more importantly, it pays for all of my releases.

By the way, you can also get a free MP3s from me if you're on that newsletter sign-up page, as there's another section for music. You can click the checkbox, I think it says instrumental guitar, and get another email with about a dozen songs that you can download. So I give away a certain amount of content for free.

If you're someone who supports crowdfunding efforts, you can go to artofworldbuilding.com/patreon. I'm on that crowdfunding site. You can donate as little as a dollar a month to support this podcast and any of my other projects as well. It all kind of goes into the same bucket.

WORLD BUILDING INTRODUCTION

Let's talk world building. If you're following along with volume 1, *Creating Life*, we will be discussing the subjects that are covered during the introduction. One of the things that we always need to decide on is our goal, so we're going to look into how to examine these and figure out what our options are.

We're also going to look at using analogues. An analogue is something that exists on Earth and we can leverage and use in our settings. For example, we might have a civilization like that of Japan and we might want to borrow elements of that when we are creating a sovereign power on another world. We'll talk about the pros and cons of how to do that and how to not be too obvious about what we're doing. Because what you don't want is to have the audience see this culture that you've created and have them go, "Oh it's just Japan. You didn't do anything original. You just stole that from Earth." So we don't want that kind of reaction.

That brings up the subject of what we really mean by world building. Now it's perfectly fine to do something like have a story happen on Earth and we do a reimagining of something like the Greek gods in modern times. You know, a story like that is fine but that is not what I mean by world building. World building is really the act of creating an imaginary world. Now I say world and we call it "world building," but more often than not, we're creating far less than a whole planet. I mean I've been creating Llurien for 30 years and I still have only two continents done at this point.

Now it might be good to have all the continents named and have some high-level ideas on all the regions, but as far as doing details of each continent, that's just kind of crazy. So that's one of the things we're going to be looking at is to figure out just how much we need to do for each situation.

I also want to throw out a general disclaimer. This will come up more when we talk about species and races, but for the most part, I use the word species throughout this podcast and the series of books. We will talk a little bit more about why later, but I just wanted to point that out now. I'm not gonna keep saying "species or races."

And on that note, if I'm talking about fictional characters we might want to invent, I'm just going to go ahead with the male pronoun "he" and not say "he/she" all the time. This is not meant to be disrespectful. It's just easier.

Throughout this podcast, I'm going to be talking about fantasy and sci-fi. Just to make sure we're on the same page, by fantasy I generally mean a world without modern technology. It can be something like *The Lord of the Rings*, where there's knights, there's castles, there's magic, fictional creatures like dragons. And for sci-fi, usually we're talking about technology that doesn't even exist yet on Earth. It might be a future state of Earth, or it might be on entire other planets like in the *Star Wars* universe, where there's no connection to Earth. But generally they have technology that we do not have.

Much of the world building advice is really applicable to both of these, but if I do specifically talk about something being for fantasy or for being sci-fi or science-fiction, depending on what you want to call it, I'll bring that up at the time, but most of the advice will cover both.

USING EARTH ANALOGUES 2

Hello and welcome to *The Art of World Building Podcast*, episode number two. Today's topic is why and when we need to build a world and how to effectively use analogues. This material and more is discussed in Chapter 1 of *Creating Life*, volume 1 in *The Art of World Building* book series.

WHY BUILD A WORLD?

Now we're going to move on to chapter 1, "Why Build a World?" Depending on your genre, you may feel that you have no choice, that this is a kind of obligation that has been thrust upon you by circumstances or even the expectations of an audience. There are ways around that.

For example, if you are writing a sci-fi story where there are characters from Earth, well then in this case you can get away with not inventing gods or species, or plants and animals or any of that stuff. If the characters are always leaving from Earth, or if they originated from Earth and they are only encountering other humans in the context of this story, in that case, you don't have to actually build lifeforms.

Now since they are traveling through space, there are probably going to be places where they need to visit, like other planets, and in that case you will probably have to invent these other locations, but again there's the question of how much detail. So you may not have to create every last city on a planet anymore than I have done in the last 30 years of working on Llurien. But you're going to be doing at least a little bit of world building.

Now if you're doing fantasy that occurs on a fictitious planet, and there is no connection at all to Earth, then yes, you do have to do some world building. That said, you can create a world that is basically Earth by another name. So you don't have to include species other than humans. This is happening in *Game of Thrones*. Pretty much everyone there is a human. You're still going to have to create places, but at least you can keep some of the world building to a minimum, especially if this is something you don't want to spend a lot of time on.

The other solution is to use public domain species or races. For example, elves, dwarves, dragons. These are all public domain. You do not have to invent these. You can just put your own spin on any of these creations. And for the most part when you do this, you want to satisfy expectations. You don't want to be presenting something that is wildly off from what people are going to expect.

An obvious example is not to call something a dwarf and then have it be taller than humans. In that case, it's partly because the word means smaller, so that doesn't make any sense, but that's not even the point. The point is that, that's not what people are going to expect.

So when using public species and races, we can put our own stamp on them but we should at least be a little bit reasonable. If we're going to make serious changes to its appearance, its demeanor and how it acts, then we might want to consider giving it a new name, and just making it our own.

THE RULE OF THREE

Let's talk a little more about using analogues. I have something I call the Rule of Three. It's more of a guideline than a rule, but the basic idea is to make at least three significant changes to an analogue. The reason we want to do this is so that people don't recognize that it's an analogue.

A good example for me is the movie *Avatar*. I thought that this was really cool, but the thing that kept leaping out at me all the time is that this is basically Native Americans that are taller and blue. I don't know how much of the culture is really from Native Americans or the imagination of James Cameron, but it didn't seem like there was much difference between the two of them.

Now why is that a problem that people recognize our analogue? Personally, I find it distracting. We never want something to pull the audience out of the story. And most of us don't want to run the risk of causing some disrespect if the audience is just thinking, "Oh you just stole that from so and so." It doesn't make a good impression and they may not respect the work we've done as much anymore.

There's an inherent problem of lack of originality when using analogue. We need to balance having used something that already exists here on Earth with putting our own spin on it. And it's not really enough to just make minor tweaks to it. You really want to make significant tweaks, so this is what I mean when I talk about the Rule of Three.

This is not something as trivial as removing the pointed ears from elves. If I were to use elves somewhere I would probably not only remove the pointed ears, but instead of having them living in forests and being obsessed with all of the lifeforms therein, I would probably change their habitat to something else.

I would also probably change their life span so that they no longer live forever or over 1000 years. This is one of the basic ideas on what an elf is.

The goal of using an analogue is to create something new that is inspired by something that has already been created by someone else or which already exists. It's much easier to use an analogue as a springboard than to just start from scratch.

NAMES

A related issue is the name that we give our invention. For example, let's say I create a horse that has an extra pair of legs and I still call it a horse the first time I point out this extra pair of legs. The reader is obviously going to be aware of this, but as time goes on, I'm just to keep referring to this as a horse. "The guy got on a horse. He rode his horse." Sooner or later, the reader is just going to forget that this horse has an extra pair of legs because I'm not reminding them all the time. You could say that you could just keep reminding them, but is it really better to keep reminding them? Wouldn't it be better to just call the horse something other than a horse and make more significant changes to that horse?

The reason for this is that, if we use another name, and we've described this animal, now people are no longer trying to imagine that it's got this trivial change. They're just picturing something that's completely different. Okay, maybe "completely" isn't the word we want there, but the change is significant enough that they see it as a different creature. And therefore they've got this mental picture, and every time we using the word to describe it, that new mental picture is what comes to mind.

But if we keep using the word horse, well, we know what a horse is. There's a kind of mental inertia to a known term that suggests familiarity, and that will basically take over our memory of the details that are different. In other words, we'll just forget that extra pair of legs.

Now if we are working in a visual medium like film or TV, this is less of an issue because the name of it doesn't come up as much, because we're not writing sentences about this. And on top of that, we keep seeing it all the time, so obviously we're looking at a horse with two extra legs. Your eyes are not somehow going to fail to notice the extra pair of legs. Now during a high-intensity team, you might not care, but that's okay because you're focused on whatever's happening in that scene anyway.

OLD NAMES FOR NEW THINGS

Another problem we can run into is using a known term to refer to something new. For example, a few years ago, I saw a movie where the characters mentioned that there were goblins that they would have to face. Now, I've heard of goblins before, I've read about them, and I immediately had a picture in my mind of what they were going to face.

It was something small, it was nasty, it was probably a little bit malformed, poorly dressed, and possibly even green.

This was mentioned and then 20 minutes later in the film, the goblin appeared. And what came on screen? Well, it was a gorilla. I mean these guys made a computer animation of a gorilla. It even moved like one. It certainly looked like one. I was a little bit surprised that they didn't have it pull out a stereotypical banana and take a bite.

Now this was so distracting for me that it took me right out of the scene. And I thought, "That's not a goblin. It's a gorilla! What are you doing? This is ridiculous." Now in fairness, they did make two changes to that gorilla. They put two horns on it and they said "oh, it loves gold." So when you saw the gorilla, it looked like it had taken its front paws and dipped them into a vat of gold and had gold on its two paws.

Well this is not my idea of a significant change. These are both superficial changes to a gorilla and calling it a goblin. This is a good example of exactly what you don't want to do when using analogue.

ANALOGUE EXAMPLE 1 – SOVEREIGN POWER

What I'll do now is just make up some analogues on the fly and discuss a starting point, and how we can modify that, and what sorts of things we might want to modify.

First we're going to take a look at modifying a sovereign power. And by that I mean a kingdom, empire, a federation, a dictatorship, and we'll just choose one from Earth and then discuss what we can do to modify it.

Since I live in the United States, I'm going to go ahead and start with this government because I'm familiar with it.

We're obviously not going to want to use the same name, but my point is that we can call a collection of states a federation or a confederation. In fact, if you remember from the Civil War, the South was calling itself the Confederacy. I go into more details about what is the difference between a federation and a confederation in volume two, but we basically have options for what we call the resulting country. And we don't have to use those words at all. For example, in the United States we don't use either of those words to describe what we are.

This is actually quite common. For example, no dictatorship actually calls itself that. They always have another name for themselves. What I'm really getting at here is that the form of government does not necessarily have to be part of the country's name. This reality is reflected in most countries that you've heard of on Earth. Canada is a federation but they don't call themselves the Federation of Canada. Similarly, the United Kingdom of England is technically a constitutional monarchy, but they don't call themselves the Constitutional Monarchy of England. But there are places that do use the type of government in the name. This is an option you have.

Let's talk about government. Most of us find this to be a bit of a boring subject, no offense to those who find it fascinating, but this will be covered in great detail in volume 2, *Creating Places*. There's an entire chapter of this, so I'm not going to go into the details now. My point is that if you live in a given country with whatever government there is, you understand how the government functions. Our understanding might be a little bit limited, but that's okay because as a general rule, readers of our stories are not going to want to know how the country functions in detail.

However, most countries that are similar to the United States have multiple political parties. Here we have two major ones: the Republicans and Democrats. This is an obvious subject to change. You might still have two major parties, but you're going to call them something else. In a world with magic, one of those parties might be magical and the other one not magical. Or you might find some other points of delineation between them.

Once you know this, you can begin giving them typical hatreds of each other, for example. This particular subject is only going to be useful to you if you are planning to write something that has political intrigue to it similar to *Game of Thrones*.

So what else can you change about a country like the United States? You can decide to represent the United States not as its current state, but as either a future state, which gives you a lot of flexibility, or as past state. For example, you could base a country of your invention on the United States in the 1800s. You may not want to do a lot research about this, but one of the major issues still going on then, of course, was slavery. You can also decide that the country is newly formed and that there is something like our American Civil War still going on or about to brew over possibly a different issue.

Another area for change is geography. What if we were an island nation like Australia? What if we were much farther north or much farther south and the kind of vegetation here was different? This would also change the basic skin color of most of the people here. Lots of people think United States is mostly white and that white people are the majority, but this is because of colonization from Europe. The Native Americans are not white skinned. The point here is that you can reverse the typical demographics that are found in the United States and have darker skinned people be the ones who are in power.

These are some basic ways that you can change and sovereign power so that it's not as easily recognized.

Analogue Example 2 – Species

Let's talk about using a typical species, such as dwarves, and creating an analogue. Dwarves are known for certain things, such as being grumpy, being short of course, living underground, and in many cases having beards. Let's look at each of these and decide whether they are really worth it and if we can get away with removing these and possibly having something new that is inspired by our dwarf.

Let's start with the beard. Is there any reason dwarves must have beards? Biologically I can't think of any scenario where this would always be happening. You can try to say that since they are living underground, that this is cold and they want more hair on their faces, but of course that only applies to the guys, not the girls, unless of course we decide that we want all the women to have beards as well.

But you know something? Even that explanation doesn't work because if you've ever spent any time underground, you know that the temperature is actually a steady constant. I'm not sure what it is, but it's way above freezing, and obviously if we can go outside when it's 50° outside and not feel our face freezing, dwarves don't need a beard to keep the face warm.

So I can't think of a habitat reason or a biological reason why dwarves so often have beards. So guess what? Get rid of the beard. This is the kind of thinking you want to do with thinking about using an analogue or creating something from scratch. Question your assumptions. This can be difficult because the hardest influence to eliminate is one that you don't even realize that you have.

What about dwarves living underground? Now in some cases, they are depicted as hill dwarves that live out in the sun, but let's focus on these mountains dwarves, as they are called. There doesn't appear to be a biological reason why they live underground. It is usually depicted as being something like a love of gold and other natural minerals that are found there. In some cases, it's a distrust of the outside world.

This latter issue is a bit problematic because, have you ever wondered where those dwarves are getting their food? Either it's going to be shipped to them by people who are willing to trade with them, or we're going to have to invent plants that grow underground. Or we can decide that they're carnivores who never eat plant life.

But even then, what about the animals? There are only so many animals that live underground. Where are they getting anything that they can eat? This idea that they can only live underground doesn't seem plausible. It also exposes them to greater risk if they are getting any of the food from outside the mountain. All you have to do to starve them out is stop feeding them.

One of the first things we want to do is not have our dwarves live exclusively underground. And those that do are probably going to have a more pleasant attitude about trading with others. Now there are ways around this. You can decide that they have magic doorways and can teleport from one location to another to something like a farm to take what they want. Or they can have their own farm where they can grow food. This place would be protected.

This kind of thinking can get us more ways of doing things that have not been done, or get us out of a problem like this. And of course it has one of the biggest benefits in that we have used a known race or species and have altered something significant about it, and turned it into something else, with a new name.

Then there is the grumpiness. It seems that if these guys are living underground and are dependent on others for much of their food, they would be more interested in positive relations with other species, not being obnoxious and hiding in their mountain, starving to death. There's no biological reason for the grumpiness unless they've all been suffering from some sort of chemical imbalance, which could be caused by lack of exposure to the sun. Now I'm not a biologist or chemist so I don't really know how that works, but I've heard about that kind of thing.

But if they are living underground I can understand being grumpy. It's not exactly the most attractive thing, looking at all these walls of stone, regardless of how well they've been carved. There's a lot of natural beauty that you're going to miss out on if you're stuck underground. The air is also not going to be as fresh. It might even be quite stale. And generally it's not the most pleasant place to be. So that could account for the grumpiness. So to some extent that does make sense.

Another thing that makes sense is their height. If you had to tunnel through the rock to create a home or a passageway, the taller you are, the more digging you have to do to fit, right? Either that, or everyone will be stooped over. So it does make sense that their height is reduced.

However, this raises another point. This is an environmental reason for short height, not a biological one. This means that if they are living outside in the wilderness like hill dwarves, then theoretically these hill dwarves would not be so short. Wouldn't they be taller than the mountains dwarves? I'll leave it up to you to decide, but the point is that now we have taken our species and made more significant changes to who they are. We might have a new species or race and we're going to need a new name for them, but we have something new!

ANALOGUE EXAMPLE 3 – ANIMAL

Let's take a look at doing an analogue of an animal. The first thing is to just choose something that you like. For example, I like cats, so I'm going to go with a tiger. Now what's good about a tiger? Well there's all sorts of things about how it's ferocious, it's big, it chases down all sorts of animals and it pretty much scares the crap out of everybody, right? If you had one of these in your house, people would think twice about coming in.

Now the problem with a tiger is that it is a wild animal, so what if we decided that we have a kind of cat that looks pretty similar and it's tamable? We can train this thing like a dog. Wouldn't it be cool if you could make it do all sorts of things? What if we could decide that it's more of a pack animal like wolves, and they will cooperate with each other?

What we're getting at is the behavior of an animal. Take an animal that you like and start changing its behavior. It can be anything that you find interesting or which might be useful for your stories. Just have fun with it.

Another thing you might want to do is change the size and the coloring. Tigers usually have stripes so obviously you don't do that. Maybe you make it all black, for example. Maybe you need to have more of a polka dot look. Just do something different from how it normally looks. In fact, the idea of a black tiger is basically reminiscent of a panther because those are often black. You can combine features of different kinds of felines.

One thing that is tempting to many people is to create these animals that, I think these have a name, where you take something like a dog's head and put it on a cat, and then add wings from a bat to it or something. That kind of thing has been done a lot and it can be cool for something freaky, but there is a bit of a risk of being a bit of a cliché there. And there might already be one that suits your purposes. I would just recommend trying to find something that's a little bit less crazy unless you are looking to create a monster, for example.

This brings up the idea that you want to think more about behavior. How do people view this animal? Are they terrified of it or do they think it's friendly? You know, we're around horses a lot and we think nothing of them, but on the other hand if we walked into a barn that was full of giant tigers, most of us would probably get very nervous, unless these were in steel cages.

On the other hand, if these were tame, we might not think anything of it any more than we worry about horses.

ANALOGUE EXAMPLE 4 – PLANTS

Let's look at plants. You may want to choose a flower that you like the look of and change its coloring, but more importantly, you might want to just decide that it is poisonous. Once you do that, you can have fun inventing ways for that poison to be created or administered. And then also figure out treatments for this, which might inspire you to create another plant that can be used to cure this.

You could also use parts of that animal you just invented and say that the only known cure for this poison is something from that animal. This is one way to start tying together the things that you create.

You can also decide that our plant only grows in certain parts of the world and we can literally just make this up. In volume 2 of *The Art of World Building*, *Creating Places*, we have a chapter on this kind of thing and the details of each kind of plant and where it grows, but I'm not going to cover that right now. The point is that we have some leeway, and we can not only decide which latitude something grows in, but that there is a specific country that it does grow in. This can be a point of contention.

For example, a poison might grow in one country but the antidote might grow in another one that is not only friendly terms. And the next you know, you've got a problem. Someone important has been poisoned in one country and their enemy country has the cure, so what do you do? This is one way to add some additional details to your analogue so that it doesn't resemble something from Earth.

WRAP UP

So now that we've looked at some specific examples of how you can create analogs, this should give you some ideas of how you can question anything from Earth while using it as a source of inspiration, and change the details to make something new. This will prevent people from immediately recognizing your analogue.

Now I do want to caution you that some things you could change might strike you as a change when the reality is that it's already like that on Earth. For example, most of us are used to seeing orange carrots, but as it turns out, carrots come in a bunch of different colors. You could create one that's yellow, thinking you're doing something new when it's not. Now most people may not realize that, because how many people know that carrots come in different colors? But the point is that it helps to do a little bit of research.

Wikipedia can do this even though that's not exactly an authoritative source, but you can gain some high-level ideas on how your analogue really is on Earth. And frankly to find out that something comes in another color, it can embolden you to just go ahead and do that on your world.

Analogues are a great way to jumpstart your creativity, so I hope that this podcast has given you some ideas. For more inspiration, check out artofworldbuilding.com.

HOW MANY WORLDS TO BUILD

Hello and welcome to *The Art of World Building Podcast*, episode number three. Today's topic is how many worlds to build over the course of our career. Is it better to build one extensive world we use for 20 stories, or is it better to build 20 worlds for 20 stories? This material and more is discussed in Chapter 1 of *Creating Life*, volume 1 in *The Art of World Building* book series.

ONE WORLD PER STORY

ADVANTAGES

What I want to talk about now is how many worlds we should build over the course of our career. World building can often take an enormous amount of time. Speeding up this process is one of the goals of this podcast series and *The Art of World Building* books. But does it make more sense to create one world that we're going to use for the next 20 years, or does it make sense to keep creating a new world each time we're going to create a new story? After 20 stories, we would have created 20 worlds. That seems like an awful lot and something that's going to burn us out on world building. One of my recommendations is to do a mix of these two. Talk about why in just a minute.

Let's first take a look at the idea of creating one world for one story. This does have some advantages. For starters, it takes a lot less time to do this. We also don't have to think through so many items. We're only going to create whatever we need for that story, not an entire ecosystem for example. We're also not going to be tied to that world indefinitely, so if we make a mistake there is something that just doesn't seem like it's a good idea, well that's okay because we're only using that for one story. And then we're going to move on.

If we have an idea that's a little bit more "out there," and maybe we shouldn't take that risk for the next 20 years because our audience might not like that, then just creating a world for one story, where we do something stranger, it seems like a better place to do this. Because if it doesn't work, well we've already moved on.

If we are new to world building, this might be a good approach because we have a lot to learn. We're going to make mistakes and why make a mistake that we get stuck with? I've been working on the same planet called Llurien for 30 years, and I can tell you I have repeatedly gone back over what I've created and eliminated ideas that were just kinda stupid, to be honest. I mean, I started when I was 16 or 17. At that age, you're going to have some stupid ideas. It just comes with the territory.

I've had to do a certain amount of cleaning up. And sometimes the ideas that I'm removing have good parts and bad parts and I'm trying to salvage something that was good while getting rid of the bad part. Sometimes this just creates an unnecessary amount of work. Maybe it would've been smarter to just starting over with a new planet altogether after about two or three years.

If we are also not sure how much we are into world building, then this can be a good way to kind of dip your toe in the water, just like in the summer when you get to a cold pool and you're not sure if you just want to jump right in. You can just stick your foot in and say, "Okay I don't like doing this." You have to find out whether this is something that you really want to spend a lot of time and energy on before you plan to do this for however many years.

DISADVANTAGES

As with everything, doing one world for one story also has its disadvantages. If we don't do a lot of detail, then this can sometimes become apparent. The result might appear to be an underdeveloped world. It also might be less interesting. We might find ourselves using any of the standard species and races, for example, like elves and dwarves that you find in fantasy. Now if you're okay with that, then that's fine, but if you really wanted to do something more than that, well, you're now kind of stuck between trying not to do a lot of world building but also trying to do something new. And if anything you create doesn't have a lot of thought behind it, then I might come across as a poorly conceived idea.

Another problem with this approach is that if we keep creating a world for each story, then we might start creating worlds that are very similar to each other just because we start running out of ideas. Creative people don't typically want to repeat themselves, so if your first world had certain things in it, you probably don't want to include them the second world, even if they might've been a good idea. And then this process starts where, each time you create a world, everything that we include in that world, we don't use subsequently in another world and it's almost like putting ourselves in a noose. The possibilities for us keep getting smaller and smaller and smaller every time we create a world. And that's not ideal.

ONE WORLD FOR MANY STORIES

ADVANTAGES

So if we're not going to create one world for each story, what's our other option? Well, the big one is to create one world with the intention of telling many, many stories on that world. This also has its advantages. One of them is that we are only creating one world and that way we are not going to be repeating ourselves. We have the freedom to just keep inventing and connecting ideas that we have just created was something that we have already created. This is one of the things that I love about creating Llurien for so many years. You know, I might've created something initially 10 years ago and now I think of something new that has nothing to do with it, but after another year or two, I suddenly see a connection, a way of bringing these together. And the result is an additional layer of realism.

Another issue is that I create the planet for its own sake. I don't create anything to tell a specific story, and the result, I feel, is that the world just feels more real. As I said a minute ago, one of the problems with creating a world for just the story that you're telling is that a lack of depth sort of makes things feel a little bit shallow and a little bit empty. And maybe just not that realistic.

If we decide to create our own species or races, we can really do a deep dive into this and create something that's very different. This can be a draw for the fiction that we create (the audience) because we've got a world that no one else has. If you use elves and dwarves, well everyone and their brother is doing that. There's nothing new about this anymore. You can put your own spin on them but in the end, it still kind of run-of-the-mill fantasy.

And I don't mean to sound negative about fantasy. I love elves and dwarves as much as the next guy, but as a creator I don't find it terribly interesting. And as a reader I kind of think, "Well, there's nothing new about this to me, regardless of what spin somebody puts on it. I already know what to expect." Now there is a comfort to knowing what to expect, but at the same time, there's a little bit of risk in not doing anything original. And the worst result of that is just doing something that is a cliché.

If your world becomes popular, not only will that be a draw for the audience, but if you become lucky, like a George Lucas for *Star Wars*, or George RR Martin for *Game of Thrones*, you might be able to get away with doing merchandising. Now of course that's kind of a pipe dream. How many people get to have action figures made of the world that they're created? But you know, anything is possible. On the other hand, if you're using all the standard species and races, well that's probably not going to happen.

DISADVANTAGES

The single biggest disadvantage to creating one world for many stories is the sheer amount of time that you to be spending doing. Fortunately, you are listening to a podcast that is based on a three-volume series of books that is designed to speed that process along considerably. I've been doing this for a long time and I have thought pretty much everything that – well, I have thought through everything within the series or I couldn't have written it – but I can give you a huge head start on doing this deep dive into a single setting.

Now if you're a game designer, you don't have to worry about this next issue, but storytellers are famous for wanting to tell stories but finding excuse after excuse to not do so. And world building can become one of these. We can spend so much time doing this that we never tell a story. And this is much more likely to occur if you are going to create one setting that you intend to use for many years because you going to tell yourself, "Well, you know, I'm gonna write all these stories here." Maybe you're just going to sit around world building instead.

One of the concerns about spending a lot of time on a single setting is also that, what if nobody likes what you've written? You know, you've got a world that you heavily invested a lot of time in and nobody likes it. Well, again, that's one of the reasons for this series.

Now another issue that you used to have to face but maybe don't anymore is that you can spend many years working on a setting only to never get a publishing deal. But today, self-publishing is all the rage. There is actually an entire industry that has sprung up around self-publishing and it's relatively easy to do. There are a bunch of other skills that you need to pick up, but since it is a possibility, at the very least, at the end of the day, you know that you can get your work out there.

On the surface, creating one setting per book may involve less effort at the time, but if we have to create a dozen worlds over the years, is that more or less work then one more detailed, reusable setting? You may want to consider a hybrid approach. And what that means is that you create one world that's intended to be used for many stories and you spend a lot of time on this. And even while you're doing that, you might create another world that's just to tell a specific story. And in those instances, you might just want to do something that's a little bit more "out there." Take your chances with the settings that are only going to be used for one-story, while something that's a little bit more mainstream is the world that you're going to be using for a long time.

DECIDING

If you're not sure how to decide, well then one question you should ask yourself is, "How serious are you about being a storyteller or a game designer? Is this something that you intend to do for many years?" If so, you might be doing yourself a favor to create the one world that you can spend more effort and make it more unique, and where that world becomes a bigger draw for your fans.

If you're not sure if you'll enjoy world building, or you've never done it before, then it's probably not a good idea to bite off more than you can chew. You might want to just start off with something smaller and see how it goes.

HOW TO FIND TIME

Now I do have one anecdote to share with you. I never set out to spend 30 years and counting working on the world of Llurien. As a teenager, I was just kind of goofing around. When I was in college, I didn't really have the time to write fiction so it was just a hobby of mine, that I just kept having ideas for this world, and I kept writing them down.

And sometimes I would to spend a few hours writing something, and I might not have even look at that for a couple years before I ran across the file.

Later in the series, we'll talk about how to keep files organized so you don't lose everything, but at different times, life intrudes and you don't have the time to write. That's a good time to be working on a setting, whether the world is going to be used for a long time, or even something strange you're only going to use for one story.

As someone who needs to do world building as part of your career, it's a good way to reclaim lost time. And it's also a good way to kind of run with an idea once you've had it, and worry about it later, how you're going to use it or where you are going to use it. It's not a bad thing to just have an idea, write it down, have fun with it, and then tweak it later. No idea comes up fully formed at the time.

WRAP UP

You should also have a sense of just how creative you are. Do you think you have what it takes to create many worlds? Or do you feel like this is kind of a stretch and you don't even have ideas for one world? In that latter case, you might want to just focus on a single world. And I think that we can do to make that process more manageable. Will be talking more about that as this podcast progresses.

Right now we're still covering chapter 1, "Why Build a World?" from volume 1, *Creating Life*, and there are a few more sections of the volume that I'm not going to talk about today. One of these is a discussion of the problem that can happen if we create a setting and then publish a trilogy of novels, for example, and then try to use that setting for stories that have nothing to do with that trilogy.

This is something that is discussed more in the book itself, but I'm not going to cover it in the podcast.

Another subject in the book is being too close to the world building that we're doing and finding ourselves tempted to jam a whole bunch of information into the story because we are too close to what we've been creating. The problem with doing this is that we are taking the reader away from the flow of the story and the action and just kind of hitting them over the head with a bunch of exposition. This is not a good idea. And one of the things that the book talks about our ways to go around this problem.

The final section in Chapter 1 talks about our influences and how much we are going to let them actually influence us. When we're trying to do something original, we may restrict ourselves from anything that we've seen before. But we can do too far with that kind of self-imposed restriction. The book just calls our attention to this kind of thing and make sure that we have true freedom to create something great.

HOW TO CREATE GODS AND PANTHEONS

Hello and welcome to *The Art of World Building Podcast*, episode number four, part one. Today's topic is how to create gods and pantheons and why this is more useful than a single, all-knowing god. As this is a big subject, the podcast will be split into two episodes. This material and more is discussed in Chapter 2 of *Creating Life*, volume 1 in *The Art of World Building* book series.

THE TEMPLATE

If you're looking for inspiration on how to go about creating gods, *The Art of World Building* series has a template that you can download that walks you through all of the things you might want to consider and decide upon. This template is something where you don't have to fill out every last section, but the different sections will give you ideas on things you might want to consider.

WHY CREATE GODS?

Whether we write fantasy or science fiction, at some point we will probably need gods. Our characters might want to pray or swear, threaten damnation, or just give thanks. That said, creating gods is optional. Maybe we don't want our characters to do these things or we just want to avoid the whole subject. But our world is arguably more interesting if we have some deities that people can refer to at various times. It creates an impression of depth that would otherwise be lacking.

IN FANTASY

Our gods could be wishful thinking, but in many cases, especially in fantasy, they are often portrayed as being real beings who take an active role and participate in how life unfolds on the world. A good example would be Zeus, who has been rumored to father children with earthlings. We can obviously do something similar with our invented world.

Gods are portrayed as the reason the world exists. It is uncommon for the world to be portrayed as a place that already existed and the gods just stumbled upon it. Normally, we often say that the gods specifically created the world or that the world was a byproduct of something the gods were doing. These options are something that we will delve into more deeply later in this episode or the next.

In Science Fiction

In science fiction, characters are often traveling from one world to another, and each of these planets might have a different pantheon or even just a single god like we have here on Earth in modern times. But the existence of gods is sometimes ignored altogether. The usual reason for this is an idea that science typically eliminates religion, but this really isn't true. Even today in our modern societies, many of the leading scientists still believe in God and other religions, or I should say specific religions.

Either way, the belief in God still exists even among our most educated people. So there's really no reason to act like, just because science has dominated a world or multiple worlds, that there isn't going to be any religion. Regardless of our technological and scientific discoveries, people often want to believe in a higher power of some kind, so science is not going to eliminate this. In fact, even on a world like Earth, there are still going to be countries that are more advanced scientifically, and as a result, those worlds might have more atheists, for example.

But there are still going to be areas that are less well-developed and are more likely to have a strong religious basis to the livelihood and even the traditions. Whether you agree with that or not, the point is that there are still going to be religions on pretty much every planet that ever exists. There's never going to be in a time in human history when religion is just wiped out. There are probably people who wish this would happen, partly because wars are often fought in the name of religions, but beliefs will persist regardless of scientific and technological discoveries.

In many cases, those discoveries are attributed to something that God set in motion and we only eventually figured it out, so belief always finds its way to account for things that we have discovered even from our scientists.

TRAVEL

In Science Fiction, one of the problems characters may face is that they have grown up in a world with certain gods and religions, and then they arrive on other planets where people have never heard of that god or religion. Some people might find that disturbing and then might want to do something like what Christian missionaries did, where they tried to convert the locals.

This is a scenario that can cause trouble, where the characters are basically interfering with how people think on that world. Their own ideas may be accepted or they might cause more trouble than it's worth. We can have our characters inadvertently get themselves into trouble by trying to talk about their own gods and religion and how life should be lived based on this. The locals might be very offended. This is a good way to give our characters an angle that causes problems in our story and adds more depth.

ARE THE GODS REAL?

Then there's the question of whether the gods are real or not. If they are, then are they happy with the species getting so much power that they can leave the world the gods supposedly created for them? Did the gods create the universe and therefore they are okay with the species leaving the planet and exploring? Or are they bothered by this? Is there another world that is ruled by other gods who are actually real, and those guys are bothered by these travelers who have shown up and are starting to try to convert their inhabitants? This is one way that we can introduce conflict for our travelers. Some of these travelers also might be bothered by arriving on a world that has never heard of their god.

In fantasy, the gods are usually portrayed as being real. One of the ways that this typically comes up is that a priest of a religion can lay hands on a wounded person and call on that god to heal them. If this is successful, there's really no getting around the existence of that god. Obviously, they are real. We might then need to figure out the circumstances in which a god will agree to do such a thing. Do they do this for anyone? Is it only the priests? Is the cause worthy? Is that the criteria for healing someone or interfering in mortal affairs?

One of the problems with gods being real is that they are all powerful, in theory. They can swoop in at any time and do whatever they want. This is problematic from a story standpoint because that is not great to have the characters rescued from a situation by a god who can pretty much snap their fingers and make everything go away. This is something we generally want to avoid and we might want to minimize the times and circumstances under which the gods interfere with mortal affairs.

We don't need to come up with elaborate reasons for this. We can just decide that, for the most part, the gods want people to figure things out for themselves. And that their chief interference is when they are trying to heal someone through one of the priests. Saving a life seems like a good reason for a god to intervene.

On the other hand, if they are always interfering in trivial matters, then this makes the gods too much of a figure in the world. We might want to do this on a world that we are not going to use very often just because we don't want to get into a pattern of the gods helping people or interfering all the time. It removes the focus from characters and puts the focus on these deities.

THE SPECIES

If a world has multiple species, then we must also decide if there is one pantheon of gods that all of our species worship, or if each different species, like dwarves or elves, worships a different group of gods. The problem with creating multiple groups of gods is the sheer number of gods that we have to invent. If there's a group of gods who created elves, for example, then it makes sense that the elves are worshiping those gods and only those gods. If another group of gods has created dwarves, the same thing applies.

On the other hand, if there is one group of gods who has created all of the species that inhabit that world, then it makes more sense that all of the species are worshiping the same gods. The elves might be more prone to favoring a group of gods versus the dwarves, who are favoring another group of gods, but we should make a decision about this.

It might be easier for us in the long term to create one group of gods, where different groups within those gods created different species or influence them, or are simply more appealing to them. That way, all of our species can be generally aware of all of the gods and devoted to subsets of those gods. But generally they'll just be aware of all of them and paying attention to them. It's a more cohesive group of gods. What we're trying to avoid there is creating so many different groups of gods that it just ends up being a lot of work for us.

Generally, we don't want to spend too much time on world building even though it is a time-consuming endeavor, so we need to find ways to minimize the work that we are doing while also creating great content for ourselves, our characters, and our audience.

PANTHEONS

Let's talk a little bit about the pantheon. A pantheon is nothing more than a mythological collection of gods. On Earth, at this point in time, we talk about a single god, but at times in our past we have had pantheons, like the Greek gods or the Roman gods. One of the great things about a pantheon is that we have more variety. Each god can specialize in a certain set of attributes that they care about and that they influence in the hearts, minds, and souls of people on the world. This gives us the ability to have a character who worships a particular god, and this provides insight on what really matters to that character. There might be other characters who worship an opposing god and as a result, we now have some conflict.

Regarding the gods themselves, we often decide that two of them are married, or that they have children together, or that they are brother and sister. This allows us to inject typical family relationships, such as siblings who often have problems with each other or they don't get along. Children often don't respect their parents. Parents are often frustrated by their children. And we can use all of this to characterize not only the relationships among the gods, but the people who follow them.

This also greatly helps us come up with stories and myths about those gods, where one person has tried to thwart the authority of another god and this has resulted in a story, which might also result in artifacts that fall into the wrong hands, like those of the species. Generally speaking, when we have these more dynamic relationships among multiple gods, it allows us to create stories. This is kind of an improvement over a single god where that god is all-knowing, and is kind of a general deity who doesn't have anything specific about them that draws one person instead of another.

INVENTING WITH ATTRIBUTES

When it comes to inventing a god, we may want to start out with a list of traits such as truth, love, hate, curiosity, greed, fear or others from the seven deadly sins, and just come up with gods who are based on a single trait or maybe related traits, and then figure out what this god is actually like and what their followers will be like. We can also use phenomenon like choosing a god of storms or war, or even death. We can also choose a hybrid approach, such as deciding that the god of wrath is also the god of storms.

Pantheons are often not organized in any particular way beyond family relationships. However, we can inject more into this if we choose. For example, we can decide that every god is associated with a season, or color, or an element. Once we have assigned one of these to all of our gods, then we might have a group of gods who are all in favor of spring or fire, for example. Making a decision like this, it is often helpful to decide that a goddess of love or passion, for example, is also the goddess of heat. By extension, she would also be a goddess of summer, right?

Once we create these associations, it adds more color and depth to what we've created. Speaking of color, this can also result from a goddess of heat, summer, and fire being associated with maybe yellow and red, which are colors we often associate with fire.

Organized by Alignment

There's another way the gods are often organized and this is by good, neutral, and evil. Personally, I tend to avoid those particular words and say something is benevolent or nefarious. The reason for this is mostly that good versus evil is an interesting way of characterizing things, but it's also a little bit juvenile, at the risk of offending some of you. Many of us don't like boiling the world down to such simple ideas. Even so, this is an interesting way of dividing up your deities.

And what you don't want is to have a world that is mostly full of evil gods versus good gods unless you're doing that on purpose for a specific reason.

A subject that is included in volume 1, *Creating Life*, but will not be discussed in this podcast is the different power levels of gods, and children, demigods, and half gods. If you'd like to learn more about these, consider purchasing the book.

Where Do They Live?

We should also decide where the gods live. Are they on the planet and they can be accessed easily? Or are they up in the clouds? Are they on another plane of existence and they can only be reached by special means? Our decision will affect how easy it is for mortals to reach them.

There is a tradition in fantasy where mortals must prove that they are worthy in order to reach the gods. Therefore, it is not terribly easy to make it there. If I were a god and I had many worshipers, as I assume I would, I wouldn't want every last person on the planet trying to track me down all the time. I also wouldn't want them trying to get me to resolve some petty fight that they're having with someone. So the cost for someone to seek me out should be a worthy one and therefore it should probably be an arduous task to reach me.

If the gods live on the world, I recommend avoiding something as obvious as a mountaintop because most people will immediately associate that with Mount Olympus and the Greek gods, like Zeus. On the other hand, a god of the sea living underwater is obvious, but that also raises the question of whether that god is trying to avoid anyone reaching him. After all, most people cannot swim underwater to incredible depths without modern technology. Is the god trying to avoid anyone trying to contact him?

If we're doing science fiction and our species has a learn to ascend to the heavens and beyond, then if this is the place where the gods are rumored to exist, then what happens when the species is able to get up there? Do they find that the gods do indeed live up there running the world, or did they discover that the gods are not where everyone thought that they were? Does this have an impact on them? Are people disillusioned and wonder, "Hey, wait a minute, I thought that the gods were up here in the clouds and there's nothing here!"

Are they having a crisis of faith as a result of this? Do the gods even allow people to achieve technological advances so that they can discover such an idea is not true? These are some things that we might want to consider.

NOT INCLUDED

The lifespan of the gods is another subject that we will not be discussing in this podcast but you can find out more by purchasing *Creating Life* and reading chapter 2 on creating gods. We also won't discuss vulnerability and whether gods can be hurt, killed, or upset in any other way.

The mythology of our gods is also very important. This includes creation myths and end of world myths. These are two of the most important stories to work out regarding our gods and how people feel about how time began, and even more importantly, how it will end. Everyone loves a good end of the world story and this is something that characters can mention at any time. It also offers a convenient way to talk about their lives and what consequences they may face when they die and are judged by a god. To learn more, check out chapter 2 of *Creating Life*

HOW TO CREATE
GODS AND PANTHEONS

Hello and welcome to *The Art of World Building Podcast*, episode number four, part two. Today's we continue our discussion of creating gods. We talk about whether they are good, evil, or neutral, and what this really means. We also discuss titles, symbols, patronage, reputation, and what items a god might have created and which could fall into the wrong hands. This material and more is discussed in Chapter 2 of *Creating Life*, volume 1 in *The Art of World Building* book series.

GODS AND ALIGNMENT

Let's continue our discussion of how to create gods. If you've ever played role-playing games like Dungeons & Dragons, you're probably very familiar with the concept of alignment, such as good, evil, or neutral. Well that's an oversimplified way of looking at people, this is one way to organize our deities. Unless we're trying to create an imbalanced pantheon, where we have a bunch of evil gods and almost no good gods, we might want to strive for more balance.

While good and evil are fairly easy to understand, the concept of neutral might need a little more examination. Does this simply mean that a god is not good or evil, or does it mean that this god has chosen a pacifist position? Does it mean that they never interfere in the lives of those who live on the planet? A god who never does anything is arguably not particularly interesting. This might be the primary reason that some on Earth have lost interest in God.

Wouldn't it be more interesting if He was still putting in an obvious appearance that none of us could deny? Certainly, more people would believe in God if we had proof that He exists. Obviously, some people will assume that various things are proof of God, but some of us don't except that, so this leaves a lot of room for interpretation, and of course, this causes various problems.

Using this as an example, it is apparent that a pacifist god might have trouble attracting more followers. Some people might even lose their faith because there is not an answer to their prayers. If we decide that a god is neutral and a pacifist, we might also decide that they have fewer followers and priests.

Something we should also consider is that gods who are evil might not enjoy being called that. They may have a worldview that essentially rationalizes their outlook. For example, a god of domination may generally believe that people need to be ruled. However, their followers might justify abuses of tyranny based on this. As a result, others might consider the god evil whether god himself my chafe at this characterization. In fact, it might not be wise to tell a god to their face, if you happen to be one of them, that they are evil.

Personally, I avoid the words "good" and "evil" in my stories because I feel like it's an oversimplification of the way people and gods are. You have to consider the mindset of your intended audience. There's an idea for younger people enjoy this simplification of good versus evil, but that more sophisticated people might roll their eyes at that characterization. No one can tell you which approach is right. Personally, I try to avoid this by using words such as benevolent, kinder, or helpful instead of good, and for evil I tend to use words like nefarious, sinister, or feared. These get the point across without talking down to the audience.

IDENTIFYING GODS

While just about every god will have a name, there are other ways of identifying them. This includes their title, their patronage, and the symbol. Example titles would be "God of Despair," "The Weeping Gods," or maybe even "The Lord of Despair." These are basically nicknames or informal titles that one might use to give an impression of what the god really cares about.

It can be tempting to give a single god multiple nicknames, but when we are writing about them in a story, we might want to use only a single one per story. I have found that using multiple names is problematic because people get a little bit confused. In general, it's a good idea to keep things simple. If you invent multiple nicknames, I suggest using the one that most appropriately applies to the situation you are describing in that story.

Gods are often the patron of some activity that people undertake. This can be a profession such as hunters or blacksmiths, or it can be something a little more general like children or even lovers. The way to choose who that god patronizes is to first look at their attributes. A god of war will choose to support warriors or maybe even knights. This is how you can use the characteristics of the gods and further develop the idea of who they are and who worships them. A god of war might patronage all warriors or be a little more specific and only focus on the knights.

Inventing symbols for our gods often very useful. These can be put onto armor, buildings, ships, space stations, uniforms, or even worn as talismans, or in rare cases, even branded into someone's flesh. The people of our world will encounter the symbols, and this is an easy way to characterize a location or person. Someone wearing the symbol of the god of war will make it clear that they're not exactly very peaceful. However, that god could also be the god of courage.

This is one way that the symbol may be misleading. One person might decide that this person is more like and not be peaceful, while another person might see the symbol and decide the individual is very courageous or at least interested in bravery. This is one way that we can use something as simple as a symbol as a way to create misunderstanding among characters. There is a tendency for people to jump to conclusions instead of asking what something really means.

This is why it's important for a god to have a reputation.

INTERACTION

Let's resume talking about reputation and the gods and how they interact with each other in the world.

The gods may have rules about this. Maybe they've reached an agreement that they are not to interfere with the lives of people. Why would they do this? Well, from our standpoint, if the gods can keep intervening, well then it's Susie them to just fix the problem that our characters are having. This is considered to be too convenient and generally is bad storytelling form. The people should be able to solve a problem by themselves, maybe with a little bit of help from the gods, such as in healing, but not with a god simply swoop in and solve everything for everybody. Such a scenario is considered very unsatisfying for the audience. It's also a little too convenient for an author or storyteller to get themselves out of a jam because they didn't plan a story.

While the gods may have a rule about not interviewing with everyone, not all the gods are going to be okay with this, or they might agree and they might decide not to follow through. There will be times when they make exceptions. In general, we may decide that it is the evil gods who decide to intervene when they are not supposed to. After all, evil gods are not considered to be particularly law-abiding, even when the other gods of the ones who invented the law.

Some of these gods might find it entertaining that they are doing things behind the backs of the other gods. Or they might be doing something for a more specific purpose, such as helping their followers to beat someone who is an enemy of another god. These gods may engage in a kind of proxy war. This means that they may help some of their followers overthrow the followers of another god whom they do not get along with. This might be done for no other reason than to simply entertain themselves.

On the other hand, if a god draws power based on the number of worshipers that have, then it might be in their best interests to make a show of strength so that they can gain more worshipers and more power. And by extension, they may defeat and lower the power of another god.

A related question is whether the gods punish anyone who breaks the law. If there is no punishment, then these laws really have no binding effect on anyone. The result might be that the gods are interfering much more than they have agreed. This certainly implies that there should be some sort of punishment. The question then becomes how do the gods punish one of their own?

An obvious solution is that the god loses the ability to influence their followers. What if a god is punished and none of the priests who call upon the god to heal people can reach the god? That means that anyone they are trying heal cannot be healed. Furthermore, the influence of that god might be restricted. This might result in lost followers. For example, if priests are calling on someone to heal an individual and the god does not answer because they can't, because they are being punished, then this may cause a loss of faith. Presumably, a god would want to avoid this out-come. This is a good punishment to enact upon them for disobeying the rules that the gods set for themselves.

Do the gods end up on trial? Do they get physically im-prisoned somewhere? If so, where might that be? This is an interesting option because their followers might try to free the god. Maybe the god is put to sleep. If so, the question arises, how does one wake that god? Is there a special mag-ic item or technology that will do so? This seems like a ripe story idea.

We can have some characters who are upset that their god was punished for doing something that they may have caused, such as calling on the god to do something and the god answers, and now their god has been punished. Do they feel a responsibility to undo this and rescue the god? What if the god is very happy with them for having done so? Maybe they dream of a reward of some kind. Or maybe they just want their god back and life to return to normal. This sounds like a story idea waiting to happen.

This is one way to invent deities and rules that produce stories. Isn't it better than simply announcing something in exposition? It's always better to tell a story that reveals aspects of our world than to simply tell the audience.

WHEN THE GODS PUNISH

While we're on the subject of punishment, what do the gods do to their species when those species have misbehaved? Death is the obvious answer, albeit not a particularly interesting one. After all, once the character is dead, that's the end. Keeping them alive offers opportunities for additional suffering and the possibility that they can be rescued by others.

A nasty afterlife is another way to go. Volume 3, *Cultures and Beyond*, will discuss creating an afterlife in more detail. But an afterlife is a great place to put this person so that they can be rescued. Or they can just suffer there for eternity. We can also think of more interesting ways of punishing someone, such as removing magical talent, wizard. We might also decide that someone in a technological setting is no longer able to manipulate that technology. This makes little more sense if that technology is biologically based, such as using a fingerprint scanner or an eye scanner, or any sort of biological mechanism that allows them to operate machinery.

Then there's the question of how long this punishment lasts. Something permanent is obviously worse but if the person is allowed to wander the world or the universe with this restriction, then this is going to put them into situations that might be uncomfortable for them. They might have always relied on this supernatural power or a technological skill and no longer have this. Imagine the sorts of problems that will result when they go to use this ability and belatedly realize they don't have it anymore. They will already know this, but in the heat of the moment, they might just forget that they can't do it anymore.

Then there's the question of why someone ends up being punished by the gods in the first place. What sorts of crimes must one commit to get the attention of a god? Destroying one of the temples seems like an obvious choice. This is a better choice than someone taking the name of the god in vain because so many people are going to do that but the gods would be awfully busy punching everyone who did this. The more serious the crime, the more likely this will attract divine punishment.

WHAT HAVE THE GODS CREATED?

Another good subject when inventing gods is to decide on what they have created. The first choice is, of course, that they have created the world and all of its inhabitants. This is a good choice and we can decide the different groups of gods created different species or races. This makes it easier for us to distinguish between the species. After all, not all of them will be worshiping the same gods.

We can also decide that each god has created various items that they typically have in their position. The great thing about these items is that they can fall into the wrong hands. If an item has a supernatural power and then the species get a hold of it, then they might be able to do things that no mortal should be able to do.

There worst case example would be an item that has the ability to create life. Now we have a species, or a member of that species, who has control of this and is doing this without approval or authorization. And the next thing you know, they might have created a monster, for example. There are less significant things that we can do that also provide opportunities for fun.

Maybe the god of greed has a goblet that allows him to drink without ever getting drunk, and the next thing you know, someone on the planet has this. The goddess of love might have an item that allows people to fall in love with her, and once someone has this, that person is able to have one sexual conquest after another. This sound like something that could cause a lot of problems and also be a fairly entertaining story. This is especially true when that object is suddenly returned to the god and the next thing you know that person has seduced people who are now very upset with him.

With some imagination and some humor, we can create some very interesting scenarios. I recommend looking at each of the gods you have created, and once you have decided on their personal characteristics, making up a list of magic items that they have in their possession. These items should have something to do with the attributes of this god and the matters that concern them. Typically, each of these items will be associated with that god. They can also be the symbol for the god.

This brings up another point that when we are inventing our deities, we sometimes need to work on different aspects of them before we come up with something else for another area of the god. We might not be able to think of a symbol and to reinvent some of the items that this god has invented first. This underscores another point, that it can take a lot of time to develop a deity that is well-rounded, so don't worry too much about it if you don't have something to decide on.

If you join *The Art of World Building* newsletter, you can download a template for how to create a god. This is a fill in the blanks form. In looking at something like this, we may not be able to decide what we want to do, but that's okay. You can always come back later and add more detail or fill out something that we haven't had an idea on.

WHERE TO START? ATTRIBUTES

We're going to conclude our discussion of how to create gods by talking about where to start. One approach is to start with a list of attributes for which we might want gods. Examples would include love or war. Once this is decided, you can also start grouping attributes. For example, the goddess of love might also be the goddess of birth or passion. They got of war might also be the god of cunning. The reason to have these additional attributes is that we can start fleshing out what this God is really concerned about. A single attribute like four is not really indicative.

For example, some people think that war is evil but other people think that it is a necessary means to an end. As a result, some might think it's bad will while others think it's okay. If you were to tell a soldier that war is evil, they probably wouldn't appreciate that very much. After all, many of them think they are doing a noble job protecting the country that they love. And this is certainly true.

The point here is that a single attribute like war can be considered evil or good. As a result, we might want to consider flushing out the idea of what this god concerns himself with by adding additional attributes that are an extension of this prime trait.

A similar example is that of birth. The god of innocence might be the god of birth because children are born innocent, but on the other hand, the goddess of passion might be considered the goddess of birth because in theory, passionate love is what leads to childbirth. What we're talking about here is that any particular attribute can be seen as either good or evil. Okay well, maybe not all of them, but many of them can be assigned to one or more gods. What we might want to do is to create this list of primary attributes and invent the gods for these, and then as we think of related attributes, we start assigning them to the gods as we choose.

If I were to create a god of passion, I might think of a set of related attributes that is different from the set of related attributes that you think of. This is perfectly okay. By doing this, we end up getting a better sense of what this god's personality really is. And the better we sense this, the better we can portray this. This will also give us a better understanding of the mindset of the characters who worship this god or who are opposed to the god.

This also set up some interesting scenarios. For example, someone might be opposed to war but appreciate bravery. If the god of courage is also the god of war, then this might cause a bit of conflict for them. They may respect aspects of the god but not other aspects. Therefore, they might not actually worship that god. Or if they do, they only do so when it seems appropriate to them. This sorted detail can add richness to the world that we are creating and make it seem like a real place with more diverse characters and deities.

WHERE TO START? ANALOGUES

Another way to begin creating gods is to start with analogues from Earth. In episode two of this podcast, I talked at length about how to create an analogue. In this case, we might want to choose a god from Earth that we enjoy and invent another god of our own invention on that deity.

However, we must be careful with this. If we choose to use Zeus, what am I probably don't want to create a similar god who also lives on a mountain and throws lightning bolts. Everyone's going to immediately recognize this analogue. I talked about this "rule of three" in episode two, the idea being that we should make at least three major differences between our version of something and the Earth analogue that we based it on.

It can be difficult to create even one god not to mention a pantheon, so using analogues is a good way to start. We can find gods that we like and enjoy the idea of, and use them as a source of inspiration. By mixing and matching ideas from different gods, we can create something new. This convenient shortcut can speed up the process of inventing gods and get us going.

HOW TO CREATE SPECIES AND RACES

Hello and welcome to *The Art of World Building Podcast*, episode number five, part one. Today's topic is how to create races and species and even when to use each term. As this is a big subject, the podcast will be split into several episodes, each as number five, part one, two or three, for example. This material and more is discussed in Chapter 3 of *Creating Life*, volume 1 in *The Art of World Building* book series.

WHY CREATE SPECIES AND RACES?

Creating a species is one of the things we can do as a world builder. It can make our work stand out from the competition more than anything else. It is also the most reusable aspect of world building because we can use that race or species over and over again. Any series of stories we create, regardless of the medium, can end up being known for the species and races that inhabit the world we create.

What first comes to mind when you think of the movie *Avatar*? The Na'vi people. elves, dwarves, and hobbits immediately come to mind with *The Lord of the Rings*. Even a film series like *Star Wars* has its Woookies and Jabba the Hutt and a multitude of other characters that we see in the background but which are never explained to us or given names or societies, but we still think of that series as having all of these creatures anyway, don't we?

So then the obvious question becomes, "How do we go about creating one of these?"

WHAT TERM TO USE?

I think the first thing we need to decide on is what we are going to call this creation: a species or a race? Let's take a look at this subject.

Especially in fantasy, audiences are used to the word "race" being used to describe the difference between a human, an elf, and a dwarf, even those these beings are very different from each other physically, not to mention culturally and in other ways.

But on Earth, none of these exist except for humans, of course. And we use the word "race" to describe the differences in facial features and skin color. In other words, here on Earth, the differences are relatively minor compared to those on a fantasy setting, where the bodies are so drastically different.

This raises a problem with the word "race." If we're using that word to describe the difference between humans, elves, and dwarves, then how can we use that word to describe differences between different types of elves. It doesn't really make sense, does it? It's kind of confusing.

This suggests that we might want to use the word "species" to describe the difference between humans, elves, and dwarves and reserve the word "race" for the differences between versions of humans, dwarves, elves, or any other being that we create.

So let's take a look at these terms and figure out whether we're being correct or wrong or just what the story is with this.

THE TERMS EXPLAINED

The word "race" has been described as nothing more than a social construct. In other words, an artificial way of trying to group different versions of something, in this case, humans. Most humans are 99.9% the same. There are no genetic differences to warrant any classification into races or anything else, for that matter.

What this means on 1 is that if two humanoids are genetically different, they would be considered different species. In other words, separate DNA means different species. Shared DNA means a races of a species.

What this means for science fiction in particular is if we have different beings originating from different planets, they are almost certainly going to have different DNA, which means that they would be different species. By contrast, in fantasy, usually the different beings are from the same planet, so it is possible for them to have shared DNA.

So how do we know if humans, elves, and dwarves have the same DNA? Well, it's impossible. Why? Because except for the humans, the rest of those are invented. There's no actual DNA for us to take samples of and send to a lab and get back some sort of report on, right?

Now we could assume that if elves have pointed ears that this means they are genetically different, but this is a superficial difference the same way that different eye shapes or noses or other things are cosmetic. They're trivial. They're not something's genetically important.

DWARVES

Now some of you are probably thinking, "Hey wait a minute. Dwarves do actually exist on Earth, so then we could do some testing." But that's just the thing about this. That sort of testing has already been done and the differences with dwarves on Earth, for the distinctive height and other characteristics are actually caused by a medical or genetic disorder, which is why those genes are sometimes passed down from parents.

However, they are not *always* passed down. What this means is that a dwarf mother could give birth to a dwarf child. By contrast, a human who's not a dwarf could give birth to a dwarf child. This is not what you'd expect in a fantasy story, We always assume that the dwarves give birth to more dwarves and that humans do not.

In fact, on that note, that would be an interesting change. Why is it that on Earth, humans give birth to both full-size *and* dwarves, but then on a fantasy setting, humans never give birth to dwarven-sized humans? Wouldn't we end up with, for lack of a better word, actual dwarves that are always dwarves and dwarf humans? How would they be accepted?

This is something I don't think anyone has ever done and I never thought of that until just this moment while describing this, but this is something that we could certainly do in our work. On the same note, why can't an elf give birth to a dwarven elf?

The reverse is also true sometimes, while we're on the subject of height, because there are, of course, gigantic humans and these are not necessarily born from gigantic humans, even though height sometimes does run in families. It's just a situation where something has happened genetically and the result is that we have someone who is much smaller or bigger than normal.

The point is that these differences are exceptions. They are not the rule. Tis is something we need to be aware of.

COMMON ANCESTRY

Now in some fantasy settings, the author will say that all of the elves, dwarves, and humans, for example, have all derived from the same ancestry. What that would mean is that they have the same shared DNA. This in turn means that they are therefore races, which would seem to be an appropriate term in this case.

On the other hand, if the gods created elves, and then they also went off and created humans, and then they later created dwarves, each one of them is being created at a different point in time, which would seem to suggest they have different DNA and are therefore different species. This doesn't have to be the case, of course. We could decide that the gods made them all have basically the same DNA, or pretty close. As the ultimate god of our world, we can do whatever we like.

THE SPECIES PROBLEM

The last point I want to make on this is that even among biologists on Earth, there is something known as "the species problem." Part of what this means is that there are over two dozen definitions of "species," so basically even the scientists are having trouble defining what one is. So if you're feeling confused yourself, apparently you're not alone. And if this isn't your field of study, to some extent, the pressure is off to get this right because even the scientist can't make up their mind. Hopefully I'm not going to offend any scientists in the audience by saying that.

So then why does the word "species" exists? Well, it's just like the word "races." We're using this to group organisms into what someone considers a logical grouping, such as cats being different from dogs.

By the way, both races and species and interbreed, producing offspring, so I've seen some people say that if you can't breed, then you're not this or you're not that. Well, that's not actually true, so don't worry about that when you're trying to whether to call your being species or races. The whole breeding thing is a non-issue.

BIODIVERSITY AND HIERARCHY

Something we should consider when trying to decide between the words "races" and "species" is the biodiversity of our creations. For example, elves, dwarves, hobbits, orcs, and humans all have two arms and legs, one head, and no tail. But if one of them has gills or maybe wings, or two heads, that's a greater degree of difference, and if it's always the case that they are this way as a result of mating, then we may want to consider that a different species.

We might also want to consider whether to use a hierarchy to denote the differences between races and species. What do I mean by a hierarchy? Well, under humans we might have Caucasian, Asians, and blacks, and Latinos, for example, but under elves we might have high elves and then we might have drow, also known as basically evil elves. Among the dwarven family, we often have hill dwarves and mountain dwarves.

In these cases, the drow and high elves are races of the elf species. The Caucasian, Asians, Latinos, and blacks are races of human species. With the dwarves, the hill and mountain dwarves are races of the dwarf species. This sort of hierarchical structure makes more sense to me personally, but you'll have to decide for yourself if this something you want to do.

On the other hand, if we call humans, Caucasians, elves, mountain dwarves, hill dwarves, drow...if we call all of them races, there's no hierarchy or structure to that at all and it's just a little bit confusing, isn't it? Maybe we can improve upon this by using both the word "species" and "races" in the appropriate context. And generally, races are a subset of species.

There's an added bonus to using the word "species" at all, especially in fantasy: people are used to the word "races" and you can pull them out of their comfort zone a little bit and make them perk up and pay more attention and just not be so comfortable with the "same old, same old" that they see in so many books and stories.

SHOULD WE CREATE A SPECIES OR RACE?

By the way, on a stylistic point, I'm just gonna go ahead with the word "species" for the rest of this podcast episode and not keep saying "species" or "races." But everything I'm saying applies equally to both.

The next thing we should consider is whether we *should* create a species. Now if you're listening to this episode, you probably already have some idea of whether you want to or not. But let's take a good look at this and decide if it's something we actually need to do or something that we just *want* to do. Or maybe after learning everything that we need to do in order to create a believable one, we might decide after all that maybe we don't want to do that anymore. Don't worry though: the whole point of this podcast and the book series and templates is to make all of this easier for you.

IN SCIENCE FICTION

In science fiction, we may have no choice but to invent our own species. Why is that? Well, because aside from the little green aliens, we don't have any public domain species that we can use. Somebody owns the Vulcans from *Star Trek*, for example. We can use that for fan fiction, but unless we're hired by the *Star Trek* universe, to go ahead and write something for them, we can't get away with publishing anything using them.

That leaves us with two options, as far as I can tell. The first of those is that we have a setting where there are only humans and there are no species of any kind besides us. Or we go ahead and create some. Given that humanity is plenty dramatic all by itself, we don't really need to invent species if we don't feel like doing so. There are plenty of series out there that don't have any, especially if the characters are originating from Earth and only operating in our solar system, for example.

However, if we have science fiction where the characters are very far from Earth, outside our solar system, but still within our galaxy, then we're probably going to have them encountering other life forms somewhere else. Otherwise we're going to end up in a situation where we have to put that story so far into the future that the only people we're encountering on distant planets and in other solar systems are other humans, who made it there hundreds if not thousands of years ago. Unless we intend on having that kind of history, which is still in our future, then we're probably going to want to invent species that our characters can run into. Either that, or keep everyone local to our solar system.

Now there is one way around that, and this can work in fantasy as well, and that is to have magic portals or something like the Stargate from the TV show, where we can get from Earth to some distant location, in either this solar system or another one, or even in a faraway galaxy, in a blink of an eye. What this eliminates is the need for extensive years, thousands of years or light years for characters to have traveled to that other planet and have set up a colony, or a civilization, and all of that to flourish for however many more hundreds or thousands of years. All of that's very time consuming in story terms. It involves creating a lot of future history. We can avoid that by having people get there much more quickly.

Now in a series like *Star Trek*, there are species who are ever present, like the Vulcans, who are in probably every episode of that show. But then there are species who only show up for a single episode, and our characters meet them. The point I'm trying to make here is that we don't always have to create a species in incredible depth. That's something we want to save for creature or species that we're going to use throughout a series. But the nature of episodic television sets us up for a situation where characters are going to be onscreen for just one episode, and we can take more chances or have more leeway with how we present them or even how much we do when we're inventing that species. So we don't always have to go overboard and create everything.

If we *are* working on a show, we probably have a lot of help in the form of costume designers and others who are going to improve on our work, even "meddle" in it or do things that we might consider destroying it, but for authors we're going to have all of that work being done by us, so we can have more freedom but we also have more work.

The scenario of having a character who's only around for one story is a situation ripe for only creating what you need. Something to be aware of though is that if we do intend to create something for just one story, we may change our minds later and decide to expand on that. And we should just be aware of what we've originally created and whether we've boxed ourselves into a corner.

For example, we may not want to make an unnecessary comments such as, "They never leave their planet." Well, if we decide to use them in context later and we to have them have left the planet, now we're contradicting ourselves. Unless we need to make such a comment in our story, it's probably better to just not make any universal statement like that.

Of course, we could decide at a later time that something happened to that planet and now they are travelers, whether that planet was destroyed or something less extreme happened where the planet just became less hospitable. With some creativity, we can usually work our way out of a box if we've put ourselves into one.

IN FANTASY

Things are a little bit different in fantasy because we have a number of public domain species or races that we can use. This includes elves, dwarves, and dragons. No one owns these. This means that no one can tell us to stop using them. We don't need anyone's permission and we don't need to pay anybody. It's great!

The problem is that since this is true for everyone, that every fantasy author in all of recorded history is using the same species. This means they are arguably overused. Now some people probably don't mind them and have never gotten sick of them and don't mind seeing the same thing over and over again, but other people might really be desiring something new. And that's where you come in.

As a world builder, you have the ability to invent a new species and blow the socks off of your audience, and have them coming back to your work more and more because you're one of the people doing something new, something different, and it's just a little more exciting than seeing the same old thing they've always seen before.

On that note, the ability to do something new means we are not beholden to anyone else for ideas. With elves, we can only present them with so many variations because if you remove something that everyone assuming is going to be there, like the pointed ears, then people are cry foul. We can get away with making minor variations, and in fact I touched on this previously in chapter 1 in a section called, "What's In a Name?"

The trick is not to shock somebody with a name that is jarring because it's so far off from expectations. I think the previous example I used was the word "goblin" being used for something and by the time the actual goblin appeared onscreen, as it turns out, it was actually an ape. This basically caused blowback for me because I kind of rejected what they were doing and saying and it also took me right out of the scene and story. I sat there mentally criticizing the movie I was watching. That is not the reaction we want our audience to have. So when we make minor changes, that's okay, but if make a bigger change, and we remove something that's expected, then we shouldn't call it what it is based on. The obvious example is a dwarf that is ten feet tall. That doesn't make any sense, so just go there.

Another issue with using the same species that everyone else is using is that sometimes it seems like we can read ten different books by ten different authors, and get ten different versions of what an elf is. Now when I was younger that sort of inconsistency bothered me a little bit, but since then I've gotten a life and gotten over that, but some people might not like that so much. This is something that caused me personally to strike out more and start inventing my own species.

What I'm getting here is, let's say there's ten different versions of what an elf is, well I couldn't figure out what version of them I wanted for the planet I was creating. I had no criteria. I had no reason to choose one over another and the indecision was one of the things that kind of bothered me about this. That, in turn, led to the thought, "Well, why do I have to use them at all?" And so one thing led to another and that was part of how I became more of a world builder and more of a species creator.

There's another point I want to make. In *The Lord of the Rings*, we have Ents and hobbits, which are both owned by the Tolkien estate, so this means we cannot use them.

However, for some of you, you've played *Dungeons and Dragons* and you have seen treants and halflings. Well what are they? They're basically Ents and hobbits by another name. I'm a little surprised that anyone could get away with basically ripping off idea wholesale and just putting another name on them, so there might be a little more to this, and if you decide to do something like this, you might want to run this by your legal team, for example, but it is an option. To give yourself some plausible deniability, you might also want to make some changes to it.

HOW MUCH TO CREATE

We should also consider how often we're going to use our setting. Something that we're only going to use for a single story may not benefit from the time and effort that it takes to create a species. On the other hand, if we're intending to use that world indefinitely, then maybe it's worth spending that time. We might want to take hybrid approach where we create a main world and put more effort into creating species, and then for standalone short stories or a novel that we're not going to follow up on, then we can just use something standard like the elves and dwarves from fantasy, for example.

So let's talk a little bit about the scope of what we invent. As mentioned, in some cases we'll want to do a lot of world building on that species, and in other cases we might want to do the bare minimum. So let's talk about what the bare minimum is. At the very least, we should decide on the physical appearance and the overall disposition that is shared across all members of the species. A specific character might go against that disposition but that's fine.

Knowing what the main disposition of all of them is helps us characterize that one person who is different.

There are also types of species such as ogres and orcs and other henchmen that usually don't get a significant amount of development. We just go ahead and do that appearance and their overall attitude, and leave it at that. We often don't see them as having a language that's well developed or a culture, and we tend to look at them as someone who is kind of mooching on the rest of the world. For example, they may not have the ability and the technological skill or intelligence to create buildings, so perhaps they are living in ruins. Species like this require a little bit less development time.

But it isn't only the so-called evil species that can get this limited time. We sometimes see another character who is basically benevolent who is also the same way. The one that comes to mind for me is Chewbacca from Star Wars. Technically, he is a Wookie, but in the original trilogy of films, we never saw another Wookie. This basically means that he had become synonymous with his species so that whatever he was, they all were, as far as we knew.

Adding to that is that he never says something we can understand. In fact, most of his characterization comes from Harrison Ford's acting ability as he reacts to Chewbacca. That's where all of his personality seemingly comes from. Han Solo is what makes Chewbacca work, and in that sense, Harrison Ford did double duty in those films. In books in could be harder to make such a character work and we're probably going to forget that the character even exists and tend to look at them as a positive henchman.

As a side note, Wookie is capitalized for some reason but your species or races should not be. That's not a title or a proper name. We only see the word "human" capitalized if it's the start of a sentence. We can also capitalize something if it is synonymous with a region that is also capitalized. For example, Germans is capitalized because of Germany. Normally, we're not going to be doing this.

Continuing with the *Star Wars* example, on film we see many other species that are just in the background. They have almost no development time to them and they will never even get a name. This would represent the extreme of doing very little work on a species.

So now let's look at maximum that we could do. This means creating a fully developed species. That means their habitat, climate, settlement preferences, appearance of the head, body, and clothing, their gods, society, language, customs, history, relationships with other species, their supernatural talents and attitudes, and the same thing for technology, and then even what their combat skills are. All of these subjects are included in the template that you can download by joining *The Art of World Building* newsletter. This will help speed up doing this and make sure you don't overlook something.

The biggest issue with doing the maximum is the amount of hours and even years of refinement and development that you're going to do. And during this process, you're going to weed out ideas you don't like as much. You're also going to be adding things. You sometimes might add something that contradicts an earlier idea and how you have to choose how to resolve this or just get rid of one. This can be a lot of fun, but the fact of the matter is, it's extremely time consuming. It also doesn't typically produce something that you can actually sell to the public in the form of a book or something, whereas working on a story does. And in fact every minute that you spend working on world building is another minute you don't spend on your writing craft or promoting a book, or even writing that book. So what does that mean? Well, it means you should choose wisely when to do this maximum.

So how do we make a wise decision? Only do the maximum when you really need to or when you are really passionate about the idea that you are working on, or if you are intending to use that idea on a setting or in a series that you are going to write for many episodes or stories or series of books. Don't do it for just a one-off. You're basically wasting your time in that scenario.

In between the minimum and the maximum is a more moderated approach. You've probably heard that expression, "All things in moderation." Well, this applies to world building, too. What does that really mean? Well, I recommend deciding on the species' habitat because that's going to determine a lot about how their bodies developed, and even where they're going to be found on your world.

We should decide whether they're willing to live in joint settlements or only ones by their species. Now what I mean by a joint settlement is that they don't simply go out and find themselves temporarily, or even permanently, living in a settlement that is mostly human, for example, but that they actually create a settlement with humans and elves or whoever else. The idea of joint settlements will be discussed more detail in *Creating Places*, which is the second book in *The Art of World Building* book series, but the basic idea is that it's a little bit unrealistic for most worlds to have settlements that are exclusively created by and for one of the species if there are a lot of species around.

The moderation approach also includes deciding on their overall disposition, their appearance, their relationships with each other and other species. Now the areas that we can skimp on for now include their clothing, their gods, characteristics like agility, intelligence, and morale, their languages, customs, history, combat, and even the details of their ability to manipulate supernatural or technological forces. Only you can really decide on what you want to create and what you need to create for your story, but this should get you some idea.

HOW TO CREATE
SPECIES AND RACES

Hello and welcome to *The Art of World Building Podcast*, episode number five, part one. Today we continue our discussion of creating species and races. We talk about their overall attitude, deciding what they look like, and more. As this is a big subject, the podcast will be split into several episodes, each as number five, part one, two or three, for example. This material and more is discussed in Chapter 3 of *Creating Life*, volume 1 in *The Art of World Building* book series.

HABITAT

If you are following along with *Creating Life*, you will notice that there's a section on habitat. One of the subjects discussed therein is this issue that comes up in fantasy especially, where we might have elves almost explicitly holed up inside their forests and only have a few of them out and about in the world. And even then, only temporarily. When the story is done, they're going to go back home and maybe never venture out again. The same idea is often done with dwarves, who seldom leave their mountain home.

This trope comes up in fantasy quite a bit but can also be done in science fiction. This is not to say that this is necessarily a good thing or what we want to pursue, but there is this idea that the humans are the ones who are everywhere in equal numbers, and the other species are holed up in one location, and there are only a few of them out and about.

Personally, I think more variety can be done and I talk about this a lot in the book under the section on habitat. This includes the idea of joint settlements, and by that I mean a place that is built by multiple species together, as opposed to mostly being built by humans and there's just a smattering of other species there. Or an elven city where it's built by and for elves and the only others that are allowed in there are on a temporary basis. We may want to challenge this idea. And the reason that I mention this is that I'm not going to discuss this in more detail in this episode of the podcast or the blog at artofworldbuilding.com, but if you want to find out more about what I have said about this, just pick up a copy of *Creating Life*.

DISPOSITION AND OUTLOOK

So what are we going to talk about? The first subject up is disposition, or the overall attitude of our species. Another word for this is alignment. Those of you who are used to playing *Dungeons & Dragons* or other role-playing games might be familiar with this. We usually say that someone is either evil or good, or neutral, whatever that means. And I think that this is something we should talk about.

I personally don't like using the words "good" and "evil" in my stories because life is more complicated than that, and our characters will hopefully be richer, too. Now to some extent that depends on our audience. If we're writing for younger people and teenagers we might want to go ahead with that kind of thing because there are people who like a simple breakdown into good and evil. As someone who is no longer a teenager, that sort of simplification tends to make me roll my eyes. Some of you hearing me say that are going to have the same reaction. Some of you are probably going to think, "Well, just get over it. It's not a big deal." But you have to decide for yourself whether that's the sort of characterization you want to do. If it is, well then you're set. If it's not, then what other words can be used besides "good" and "evil?"

These other words get across the same point without making our audience feel like we're talking down to them. Two of the words that I resort to a lot are "benevolent" for good and "nefarious" for evil. But we can get across the same idea without even going that far.

For example, I could just say that something is violent, uncivilized, uneducated, and just is generally not welcomed in society and that gets the point across. By contrast, a benevolent species would be part of a society and law-abiding and just generally thought upon fondly. This is not to say that no one will dislike them, but if they are living among the population and a character's making minor complaints about them, that gets across that they are not really that bad. They're not murderous. They're not thieving all the time. Even saying that they feel uncomfortable around that species because they don't understand the customs or something like that, or like the food, gets the point across that they are around in the society but there's something about them that people don't like, or at least this character doesn't like.

That sort of characterization can be a lot more helpful than just calling them benevolent or nefarious. It paints a more vivid picture. It also gives you the opportunity as the writer to have two characters argue about that species, with one of them saying negative things and maybe the other saying positive things, like, "Hey, they're not that bad. They did help us with this, that, or the other thing." One of them can say, "Well, if you don't like them, then why do you wear a piece of clothing that is inspired by them?" This could in turn allow us to observe that many people do that sort of thing and that this character didn't think it's a big deal. It is not some sort of endorsement of that species.

We can also say that the particular species doesn't mingle with everyone else. They've got their own special quarter like the French Quarter in New Orleans. But maybe it's the Elven Quarter or Dwarven Quarter, and that this is one of the reasons that some people resent them. If we feel like someone is not mingling with the rest of us, we tend to assassinate their character. It's not great but it's something that humans do.

So we could decide that if the elves are living apart from everyone inside the settlement, that does say that they are welcome here but that maybe the elves are the ones doing a little bit of shunning, and that people will say that, "Well, they think they're too good to eat our food, or to live among us." It's a way of getting across that they're part of the settlement and the life there and maybe the culture, but there are still people who don't like them, even though they're basically a benevolent species.

By contrast, for an evil species, people can say that they are not allowed here or that they haven't been inside since the last attack however many years ago. Or that maybe some knights are riding out of the city gates at some point, and are on the way to deal with some sort of uprising from the species. This still gets the point across that this is not a pleasant species. It's more vivid. And this comes across better than just saying, "they're evil."

We can also make this point by describing the city layout, the walls, the guard towers, and the types of defenses that exist because some of those will be designed to repel that particular species. There might also be special weapons that individuals have. For example, someone could have a knife and say, "I use this to twist out the hearts of those little bastards."

These are some alternatives to ever using the words "good" and "evil."

GOOD VS. EVIL

This discussion on good and evil brings up another point I alluded to earlier, and that is that humans, at least, are a lot more complicated than that. Now we do have some people that we have traditionally decided are wholly evil, such as Hitler and maybe Saddam Hussein, and by contrast, there are people that we've decided are basically good. Mother Theresa would be an example of that. Without getting into the specifics of any of those people or anyone else, most of us are not wholly good or evil. We're a mix.

However, people tend to oversimplify things and this is where that good vs. evil idea comes into play. I don't want to get too philosophical about this because that's a whole other subject, but there are people who believe and will say that mankind is basically good and that something has to happen to make someone go evil, or something happened to them when they were born, something was just off, or wrong. We usually want an explanation of some kind for why that person has done despicable acts.

And the types of acts we're talking about here are obvious crimes like murder or rape. These are atrocious enough that it makes it very easy to say that this person is evil. But what about much more minor things like a traffic infraction or, well, I don't want to say that driving drunk is minor because people are often killed from that, but there isn't the intent to kill. Then there is smaller stuff like cheating or telling white lies. The point is that evil comes in different degrees of how awful it is. So even if we decide that a species is evil, we should have some idea just how evil they really are.

Is their big crime that when they drive cars, they never use their turn signals? Or do they go around murdering people? In the latter case, yes, we would just call them evil. In the former case, we might curse about them but they're still going to be a member of society and they might get some tickets, for example, but we're probably not going to consider them evil

UNIFORMITY

More to the point, we can have one person who does go around killing people and another who never does. Or at least, they only do it in self-defense or as part of law enforcement or the army, for example. The point is that we can have two members of the same species where one is basically good and the other is basically evil, so that there isn't a uniform way of looking at all of them, just like with humans. This is arguably the single biggest reason not to go with that sort of characterization.

Is it realistic for most of them to have the same disposition? Unless we can think of a good reason, my answer to that would be no. After all, why would they all be the same? Did some magical event create all of them and then somehow infect all of them so that they have a certain nasty attitude? Because that would explain it. They could be a species that developed society far later than humans and as a result of this, they are considered kind of barbaric and are treated like third class citizens. This could, in turn, give them a healthy attitude that makes them be uncooperative and essentially evil. That's another justification for them being this way.

Especially in fantasy, we could decide that gods who are basically evil are the ones who created that species and as a result, that species has inherited the disposition of those gods. This could explain them being evil. For example, I've been creating the world of Llurien for about 30 years now. There are seven species, each one created by a different group of gods. The gods of greed, deception, jealousy, and fear created one of the species, called daekais. This species inherited the combined attributes of the four gods who created them. These attributes heavily influence their outlook so you can imagine that they're basically one of my evil species. I don't need to say that all the time. I can get it across in other ways, but that's how I set that up.

And one point I would make there is that I decided that those species are heavily influenced by those attributes but they are not incapable of other ones because that would be too limiting. This arrangement has a side effect of making most of the daekais have a relatively uniform disposition. This means the other people on Llurien, like the humans, know what to expect from one of these, and as a result, they have a predictable reaction. This causes daekais to be largely shunned and not welcomed in society. They are also feared if encountered in the wild.

What this is good for is that my characters have something for them to be afraid of and try to avoid when they are traveling. However, it also caused a problem. I can never have this species of daekais living in a civilized society because no one would ever accept them, and this makes them very limiting. I don't know about you, but I don't really like having limits on my work and my opportunities when I'm writing, so what did I do about this?

The idea of a curse or something magical (or even technological in science fiction) creating an alternate version of a race of species is a basic idea that has been around for a while. So basically I have another version of them and they go by another name: morkais. Now if you notice my naming convention, one of them is called daekais and the other is morkais. So the species is kais, and then the two races are morkais and daekais. This allows me to make universal statements about all of kais and then universal statements about daekais and more such statements about morkais, where those statements are differing.

Now you could say that I've just duplicated my problem. Instead of one race with a uniform disposition I have two of them that are in opposition to each other. This is a fair criticism. However, it does get me out of the problem of having kais that are never part of a civilization because the morkais are allowed to be there and the daekais are not, so I at least solved one of my problems.

Now there's still another problem in that people know what to expect and have a certain reaction to each one of them. The easy way around that issue is to have both races look physically identical. Therefore people don't know which one they're actually dealing with. This allows one to masquerade as another for infiltrating somewhere they're not allowed to be. It also causes some people who are short on faith to not trust either member of that species. This can cause everything from minor interaction problems, where there's just some distrust being exhibited or even said out loud, to outright accusations of crimes that a morkais, for example, would never do as a good species, but a daekais would, and someone is trying to say, "Well, that guy's a daekais pretending to be a morkais. He's actually this evil kind of person who would do this horrible thing that I'm accusing them of."

Each race of this species could be aware of this problem and either try to minimize it or use it to their advantage. For example, the benevolent morkais might try to never give the impression that they have the character traits of the daekais race, so that no one accuses them falsely. This could make them feel that they have to tiptoe around suspicious humans, for example. This in turn might make morkais a little bit annoyed with humans because they're the ones who do this sort of thing. Maybe humans are the only ones, but maybe not. As you can imagine, if you were a benevolent morkais, and you had to deal with people assuming you're a daekais and up to no good, this might make you have a problem with the daekais as well, so that you want to participate in eradicating them or doing something to minimize the distrust with which your race ends up being viewed.

So now we're ending up with a much more varied situation when it comes to the disposition of this species, rather than just saying they're all the same.

OTHER MEANS TO VARIETY

Another option is deciding that some of them are corrupt. For example, we could take a benevolent species and then have a certain group of them run across some sort of evil magic item or technology that somehow corrupts them and they are permanently turned into a more nefarious version of that species. This also gives us an entry in our history log of things that have happened in the past because this would presumably be a famous incident. It can also help us create an artifact, whether it's magic or technology.

We can also decide that this was an accident or that someone evil did it on purpose. Or if it was a previously evil species and now there's a good race of them, we might say that someone was trying to save them and they were a do-gooder who wanted to make the world a better place. And it worked, but it only worked once. Then we just have to decide how many of that group are there. Are there a couple dozen or an entire society? Has it been ten thousand years and that group has spread across the world and there are different colonies of them everywhere?

All of this gives us options for deciding on the disposition of any species we invent. And more options is good.

APPEARANCE

Let's continue talking about the appearance of our species or race. The ability of two races of one species to masquerade as each other is a great thing. But it's certainly not the only thing we should consider. However, we probably do want to make a decision about whether we would like that ability before deciding on creating two races (of a species) that look so different from each other that there's no way this could happen.

One reason to go ahead and make them look the same as that it's a lot easier to create just one appearance than two. Whether we like it or not, people do judge everything based upon appearance. While this is certainly a human behavior, we find it believable that others do the same thing. Now we can take a physical feature and assign any sort of traits that everyone. One culture might decide that something is a negative while another might decide it's a positive. We should probably think of a reason for this.

For example, there's an idea that you don't wear white after Labor Day, at least here in the United States. Therefore, someone wearing white after Labor Day is considered socially and fashionably clueless. This might make some people mock them while other people might have no idea that a fashion faux pas has occurred. While this is a clothing example, the same idea can apply to parts of the body. For example, someone could decide that having large hands means you are generous, or they could decide it means you like to steal things. This can be spun either way.

If we have a species with wings, and someone's wings are shorter than most people, we can decide that they're deficient in some other way. If the species prides itself on its sense of smell and some of them have large noses, then this could be a positive. There were times in human history where larger women were considered more desirable because they were seen as better child bears, but today we're all about the slender woman being more desirable.

Something all of this is alluding to is that culture can have an impact on how we view a feature. A great thing for us as world builders is that we can largely make these up. We can decide that a species typically has a certain feature such as a large nose and that certain members of that species do not, and now we have a comparison for characterization. So part of what we're trying to decide here is what is typical of the species or race? We need to know this in order to decide that a certain character from the race is somewhat different from the norm and has been judged this way or that.

We should also decide how clean the species tends to be. For example, if they are generally messy but our character is neat, maybe that person gets more respect from other species. And what does that say about him? Do his own kind find him arrogant? Does he care what they think? And why is he like this? Maybe he aspires to be better than them or he just feels the need to keep others suspecting that this character is bad, because we sometimes do that to people. Maybe his appearance gets him some opportunity.

The reverse can also happen if a species is typically neat but he's a sloppy person. Maybe his own kind think he's a slob and they don't want anything to do with him. Maybe another species thinks he's more down to earth. We can decide he is too busy to care about his appearance, although this is a cliché, or we can just decide that he's either clueless or indifferent. Either way, knowing how people in the species typically look allows us to characterize him. And this is always better than having no reason to decide a character is one way or another. If we just can't make up our minds, this gives us a decision point. And quickly making decisions is good.

ARE THEY HUMANOIDS?

One question we should tackle is whether our species is going to be humanoid or not. If so, then it's pretty easy to decide that they have one head, two arms, two legs, and the usual other parts. But if they're not going to be humanoid, then this raises other problems, one of those being that they can't exactly masquerade as humanoid. The ability to shape shift could solve that for us, however. If that ability is not innate, we can give them a magic item or a technological one to do so. However, that still makes this ability somewhat rare.

Another issue here is that accommodations and eating utensils will be different. Maybe they cannot sleep in a normal bad. Maybe there are no places for them to stay when the characters are traveling, such as an inn or a tavern. They may have to sleep outside. They also may not be welcome inside.

One point here is that you will have to make additional considerations when writing for this non-humanoid species. You might have to do more planning in order to include one of them on a trip. If you have something like a giant spider, it's not going to be able to get on the back of a bird or flying unicorn, for example. If your dragons are big enough, then it might work. Even a regular sized spider might be an issue, but at least they have an easier time getting around. This is a subject we're going to have to put more thought into it if it's a non-humanoid.

In a non-visual medium, it might also be challenging to quickly and successfully describe what this race will look like. We might think that we've got something good because we're picturing it, but we don't do a good job of describing it and the audience struggles. In other words, there can be more risk to this. Decide whether it is worth it and whether you really want this to be that way. What purpose are you hoping to achieve? And do you care about the limitations that this is imposing on your stories?

FACIAL FEATURES

When it comes to describing facial features, we want to once again decide what most of the species or race looks like. However, just as humans can look different from each other, we might want to create variety. The only problem with doing this is that it takes time. We will want to consider everything about the face.

For example, the overall face can be round, oval, square, or heart-shaped. We also want to consider the brow, eyebrows, eyes, the iris, cheekbones, noses, mouth, teeth, and chin. In *Creating Life*, I've got a handy chart that you can read that shows you all of the options for these. However, one of the issues that it does bring up is that we sometimes cannot use the Earth name for something. For example, we have the Roman nose and the Cupid's Bow. These are both referencing something on Earth. If our story is taking place on a world that has no knowledge of Earth, we can't call them that. Our choices are either to omit it altogether or come up with another name, or just describe the feature.

One problem with inventing the face is that we could come up with features that sound like they work together but when someone actually draws them, they don't work. But there is a way around this. I have found some online programs that I have used to create an avatar. What they can allow you to do is create a whole face. There are examples of this on artofworldbuilding.com but you can also go to pimptheface.com and try it there. And you can use another one called faceyourmanga.com. With these free programs, you can just experiment and have fun and not worry about it too much, but it can also spark ideas. And it's pretty easy to swap out the facial features.

THE BODY

Our body design work is largely done for us if we are creating humanoids. The first decision we're going to want to make is how big they are compared to humans. If we are creating multiple species, we will probably want to create some that are smaller than us and some that are bigger. The differences can be large or small. Maybe we have a 9 foot species and a 3 foot one. Or maybe they're only 7 feet tall and 5 feet tall, so pretty close to humans.

One of the things that this will affect is how formidable a species is in combat. Something big tends to be stronger. It might also have a harder time sneaking up on people as opposed to a much smaller species. Now when I say formidable, there's no reason that a smaller species can't be deadly. For example, I have one that tends to swarm like bees. They are certainly intimidating to anyone who runs across them. In fact, there are actually more intimidating than some of the larger species. Even so, you will note how I use the swarming technique to make them ferocious whereas the larger species don't need that kind of help.

Another issue here is the clothing. A smaller species might not find clothing suitable for them if they are trying to steal from a larger species or vice versa. They might have to steal from children. On the other hand, a 9-foot-tall species will not have any options for this, or at least, not unless there's some other tall species. If they're incapable of the sort of industry that makes clothing, then maybe they are typically seen without it. Or maybe the clothing is very rudimentary, such as a cloth potato sack, for example.

If a smaller species does go around stealing clothes because they are not capable of making it, then most of what they have is probably going to be mismatched. This is a quick way to imply their lack of sophistication. We don't actually have to tell the audience that they can't make clothing. We can just show this. And if they can't make that, there are probably also other things they can't make, including weapons for their size. They can once again steal something if it's appropriate, such as using a human short sword as the longsword, or if they are a truly large species, they may have no weapons that they can use except for the two-handed sword. Maybe this results in a fighting style that is largely brute force, using something like a club that is essentially a tree branch.

There is another option here as well. There could be people who design weapons for these larger creatures, even if maybe they shouldn't have them. Who would do this? Well how about your evil overlords? And with that, we bring ourselves full-circle back to the subject that we started this episode with: good vs. evil.

I hope this is giving you some ideas. Our next episode will conclude our discussion on species and races.

HOW TO CREATE SPECIES AND RACES

Hello and welcome to *The Art of World Building Podcast*, episode number five, part three. Today we conclude our discussion of creating species and races. We talk about their gods, characteristics, relationships and more. This material and more is discussed in Chapter 3 of *Creating Life*, volume 1 in *The Art of World Building* book series.

CONTRADICTION

As usual, I'm going to use the word species rather than continuously saying species or races throughout this episode. All of the advice applies equally well to either. If you've been following along with this podcast, we've already discussed gods in the previous episode. What we want to look at now is the species and how their gods can impact their lives. We don't need to have already invented our gods, although that is certainly an option.

In my experience, it doesn't really matter which one you do first because there's going to be a lot of crossing back and forth between species, gods, and the world, and altering things continuously as we build up what we're doing. Refining our vision is an inherent part of world building. Few people ever get a correct right out of the gate because there's so much work to do and it will take weeks, months, or even years of work. Some ideas stand the test of time better than others.

We also almost certainly want to expand upon an idea as we go along. So some of the advice in this section may flip-flop between assuming you already have gods and are now trying to decide which ones your species worships, or that you're creating a species first and are going to add the gods after the fact. It doesn't really matter as long as you make a good decision.

Saying that reminds me of the expression, "it seemed like a good idea at the time," but it's just part of the process that we sometimes change something that wasn't working out after all. Or if we have a better idea and replace something. The only time you're really stuck with an idea is if we have already published it. However, this depends upon your ethics, for lack of a better word. There are certainly authors who have released a product that has contradicted a previous release. You can do this, too, but be aware that people tend to have a pretty good memory and will catch you on this. It really depends on whether you want to be known for being consistent or not. Rabid fans won't care and will just love everything you do, but more casual fans will unfortunately feel some disrespect for your world building if you contradict yourself a lot, so just be careful.

One of the ways to avoid contradicting yourself is to keep everything written down in a file and have a system of files or even spreadsheets where it's easy for you to refer to everything and make sure that you don't contradict yourself later. This is infinitely more effective than just relying on memory.

So let's get into talking about gods and species.

YOUR SPECIES' GODS

Whether we have the gods or the species first, one of the things we need to do once we have both of them is to align their characters. In episode 5.2, we talked about the concept of good versus evil, and I'm just going to use that terminology here for the sake of simplicity. There is a tendency to decide that evil species worship evil gods and good species worship good gods.

And this makes sense. A species that tends to go around murdering people is probably going to worship a god of murder if one exists. This is a little bit simplistic but it makes so much sense that it's kind of hard to ignore. And I feel like this is one of those areas where we can be a little bit predictable and no one's going to cry foul.

But what gets a little bit more interesting is if we have a god of good fortune and we have these murderous species also worship that god. Now why would that happen? Well, if I was going to go murder someone, I would certainly hope that my attempt to do so would go well, so maybe I would also worship the goddess of good fortune. Now that god or goddess of good fortune might not answer my prayers, but then again, who knows, we can make things more complicated than they appear at first.

The question that this scenario raises is whether this god of good fortune actually cares what sort of act is going to take place before deciding whether to bless that act. At first glance, it seems obvious that a god would care. After all, they don't go around blessing every last action, right?

At the same time, I'm not going to ask that god to bless everything that I do. If I'm at dinner and reaching for the salt, I'm not going to ask the god of good fortune to make sure I don't knock over a drink while I'm doing so.

Of course, I could do that, but if I was the god being asked for trivial things all the time, I would probably tune it out, wouldn't I? So it's reasonable to assume that the gods do pay attention to what's being asked of them. Is a god of good fortune going to bless someone who is going to murder someone so that the murder takes place? Well, you're going to have to answer the question for yourself because it's going to depend on what you're doing, but for a normal scenario, we would probably say no.

At the same time, if the god of murder is watching and trying to decide whether to let something happen, maybe that god doesn't want a certain person murdered and therefore thwarts the murderer. Now we don't need to discuss every last scenario because there are so many things that we would be sitting here for the rest of our lives, but the point I'm making is that gods are going to be paying attention to what is being carried out and decide whether it happens or not. And by the same token, the species are going to choose gods to worship based on the way that species is in general and of course the way that individual member of that species is.

Obviously, to determine this we have to have this worked out. For the rest of this discussion about this, I'm going to assume that you already know the dispositions of the gods and your species. That said, if you don't, this is an opportunity to invent either the gods based on what your species are actually like, or the opposite of this. Now if you already have your species but you don't have your gods, it can be relatively easy to invent gods that you imagine your species worship. Especially if you are new to world building, this might be the way to go. And even if you've been doing well building for a long time, you've probably created a lot of gods, and at this point you might feel like you're just out of ideas.

On one hand, we don't want to be redundant, but on the other hand, it makes sense that every world is probably going to have a god of war or god of death, or some of these basics. So when it comes to the gods, we don't need to go crazy looking for a variety. It's more when we're inventing a new species that we want to do a species on one world that is very different from a species on another world that we've invented, because otherwise that will stand out as us stealing our own idea.

In that sense, you might want to put your priority and your focus on your species and their character, and its behavior, and make that unique, and then invent your gods to the species. So let's assume you already know what your species is like. Well, it becomes relatively easy to invent deities that have something to do with the species. Not only do characteristics play a role in this, but so does their culture. If our species tends to live somewhere very humid, then maybe they focus on a deity that has something to do with the weather.

This is also true if they are heavily into agriculture because the weather is such an important part of that. This might also be true if they spend a lot of time outdoors because they are not sophisticated enough to build settlements and they therefore have no other choice but to either live outside or to take over abandoned settlements, and those are only going to be so well-kept obviously. Exposure to the elements is going to make the species care about the god who deals with those elements.

A warlike species is going to care a lot about gods who are involved in war. This can be everything from the god of war to a god of skill or accuracy or virtues like knighthood. Well, that's not a virtue, but the virtues that go into knighthood. On the other hand, if the species tends to be very peaceful, then they're probably going to be paying more attention to a god of peace, for example. Some of this is fairly obvious, but I'm just trying to give you basic ideas you can start off with and then refine as you go along.

What can really bring our species and our gods more to life for us and make it more vivid is when we find contrast like the one earlier about a species that tends to murder people but also worship the goddess of good fortune. This kind of contrast makes them more interesting. This sort of contradiction is a little bit easier to do if we already have our gods created first because one of the things we'll end up doing is looking at our gods and, we'll have a list of them and see all the things that they care about, and we'll have our species, and we'll keep thinking, "Well, which one does this species pay attention to?" And obviously they could worship more than one.

But let's say we decided on a couple obvious ones and are looking at the list of other gods and we're thinking, "Well, is the species really going to ignore all of these gods?" Well, that can get us into thinking about more interesting ways that we can find to associate them with a god. And the best advice I can give you for that is to have s list of deities and compare them. Think outside the box. Find another way to associate them with someone.

As mentioned in the previous episode, one of the ways that I did this was that I took a group of four gods and I merged them together into one sphere, as I called them, and this was done for reasons that had nothing to do with the species. It was done for the gods, but then I decided that these seven different spheres of gods had created my seven species on my world of Llurien. I also decided that, because a group of four gods had created a species, that the species was heavily influenced by those four gods. And this really helped me determine what the species are like.

And of course it made it obvious which ones among the gods they paid more attention to. This is one of the benefits to having organized your deities. They can essentially do some of your work for you.

SPECIES CHARACTERISTICS

Since we're talking about characteristics, let's continue with that. Anyone who's ever played role-playing games has probably seen a list of characteristics like intelligence, wisdom, charisma, strength, constitution, agility, dexterity, and morale. This list provides an easy way to start thinking about what our species is capable of. This is one of those things that we might determine for our private files but we never mention to the reader. What it gets us is thinking about what they're like and making a quick decision.

What I typically do is use a scale from 1 to 10 with 1 as worst and 10 as best. And I just quickly make a decision. I don't spend five minutes thinking about whether the agility is a seven, eight, or nine. I just pick a number and I go with it. Obviously, I'm never going to tell the audience this, and even for my own purposes, it's not enough.

What you really want to do when you choose a number like that is just quickly do that at first to get some sense of what this species is good at and what it is not good at. What we want to do next is write a sentence or two describing that ability. If we've decided that the intelligence is a nine, we don't want to just write that they're very smart because that's kind of obvious. What we want to do is describe that intelligence.

For example, we could decide that they're very good with book smarts so that they're very good with architecture and sciences, and technologies in a science fiction setting. As a result, they're one of the species who invent things. They will most likely be respected for this intelligence and their abilities. Now we're starting to get into their relationships. Obviously, what we're doing is starting to flesh out what they're like based on this attribute.

For intelligence, we could also decide that this means that they are formally educated. They are not only the kind who attend universities but also teach at them, and author scholarly books and treatises, and anything we associate with higher learning. This in turn might mean that this species in general is relatively well-off. Since they are well-educated, then they are probably the sort who are in charge of governments. After all, there is often a "pay for play" kind of thing going on where the wealthy are the ones who end up in charge. We certainly see this here in the United States where I live, where there is almost an oligarchy of people who are wealthy running the country.

The reverse can also be true if we've decided that they've only got a three for intelligence. This implies that they are not educated and that they didn't have industry and that they are probably relatively poor as a result of not being able to hold down high-paying jobs. This might also lead to things like more crime from them, if they're trying to improve their lives in ways that are not legal.

This might also affect their morality, which is another one of the characteristics that I listed at the beginning. They may have questionable morality, which is not to say that those who are very intelligent have great morality because they might also be correct. Actually, you know what? I misspoke. I mentioned morale before, not morality. Even so, the advice still holds.

But while we're on the subject of morale, this is something that will come up in combat, and arguably those of us writing science fiction and fantasy are going to have characters who end up in fights. Morale is basically an indication of whether somebody runs away or stays and fights, even if the odds are not great. Once again, we're talking about the characteristics of the species as a whole, and that allows us to determine if a specific character is someone who upholds that or who defies it.

Wisdom is another of our characteristics. The wiser people may be someone who is an advisor to the court, and the species could be known for this. They may either be the person in power or someone who advises them. An entire species can be known for this. They may also have decided to live a peaceful, humbler life where they eschew that kind of thing. Maybe they just tend to be farmers who are out in the country. Such a characteristic combination is something we're going to make up as we go along.

Of course, it's possible that these wise characters are the ones who are philosophers are writing important and influential papers and are therefore sought out and they might also be teaching at universities. They may or may not be religious. It really depends on how we spin that.

Charisma is another one of our attributes and can affect everything about this person or the species. They could be someone who's very charming and is therefore good at being an effective politician who rises to power. Or they could be someone who has more street smarts and has more luck charming people on the streets. This is its own kind of wisdom. It's emotional intelligence.

The charisma also takes into account the physical features of a species. A species we find physically unpleasant would not be very charismatic to most of us, and vice versa. Do you see how it's not enough to simply say that they have charisma? We really need to qualify that. This is where a sentence or two comes into play. We're not just giving a number for charisma like eight. What we want to do is explain the number that we assigned.

PHYSICAL CHARACTERISTICS

Let's move on to some physical attributes, like strength. This is something that's pretty easy once we've decided what the body is like. It doesn't take that much thought. However, we can decide that while the species is kind of slight of build, that they have some sort of unusual strength. Maybe they frequently fool people into not expecting that. We have a certain amount of leeway here because no one from this world is going to show up and say that the species can't really lift something that's a certain number of pounds.

Then there is constitution. This is an indication of how hardy they are and how much endurance they have. We may decide to take the physical appearance into account when deciding this. For example, if we have a species that's only 3 feet tall, then when they walk from one place to another, it's gonna take far more steps for them to get there than someone who is twice their height. We may decide that they have more endurance so that they can travel the same distance, maybe not in the same amount of time, but they might reach a place in 10 hours instead of 6 or 7 hours, but they still get there in the same day. What I'm getting at here is that we can use constitution to compensate for this.

Then there's agility and dexterity. Both of them are and a measure of how effective they're going to be in combat. Dexterity is going to affect the ability to manipulate anything with their hands. A musician would have a higher dexterity. In our world, we may decide that magic requires drawing elaborate symbols in the air or manipulating things in complicated ways with the fingers, and that this therefore requires dexterity. Assigning our species and low dexterity might mean they cannot do these things. They might also lack refinement affecting their ability to use something like a sword so that they end up using a more brute force weapon like a club.

That brings us to agility. If they have a high agility, then these might be our martial artists. If they have a low agility, then probably not. Having decided this will impact our decision on how they perform combat.

When it comes to getting started with making up some characteristics, we probably already have some basic impression of what they're like. Next we just want to list these characteristics, assign a number, and then begin thinking about how to flesh out those with a few sentences that help us determine what they're like. The number is just a starting point and something that we're never going to tell anyone.

WORLD VIEW

Let's talk a little bit about the world view of our species. One of the problems we can face as world builders is that we might have only lived in one place for most of our lives. The result is that we have a certain worldview and we may assume that the rest of the world has a similar worldview even if we know better. The end result is that we might assign that worldview to our species. There's nothing wrong with this, but if our audience is from the same place, then we're basically presenting a fictional species just like humans. This is a mistake we should try to avoid.

Now if we had the chance to live in different parts of the same culture, or different cultures for an extended period of time, we may have a better understanding of the world view of different places. If our own assumptions about worldview have been questioned, this makes a little bit easier to detect the kinds of things that we might want to change. But without that, what do we do?

We can force ourselves to question everything. This can be difficult and there is no shortage of fictional species who are basically humans by another name and with a different face or appendages, or something similar. Personally, I tend to think of this as a failure of imagination. That's not the kind of reaction we want, right? We'll look at this a lot more in *Cultures and Beyond*, which is *The Art of World Building* volume 3 and some of the episodes there, but I wanted to touch upon this now.

One of the things we should want the most is for someone to react differently to things that we do. There are a lot of clichés that we can run afoul of even when we are writing for human characters on Earth. We certainly don't want fictional species to react the same way as us.

For example, there is the innocent rant, as I think of it. This is when someone says something like, "You gonna kill all of these innocent people!" And the evil character says, "Innocent? They're not innocent!" And the bad guy starts going off about how no one is innocent. This makes me roll my eyes when a human is doing this, so imagine a fictional species is doing that. We really need to avoid that.

Originality in the world view is going to be a lot more important than originality in what they look like, especially if you're working in the TV industry because there's probably someone else who is going to go ahead and design that species on screen, as far as their appearance goes. As a world builder, I think the most important thing we can focus on is the worldview of our species. One way to do this is to think of cultures on Earth that are different from the one we lie in and borrow ideas from them.

For example, we had the Vikings. They were known for being a seafaring power back when oar powered ships were the rage and we hadn't really gotten that good at wind powered ships. They also did a lot of conquering. They were thought to be very fierce and strong. And they had a love for mead. None of this is their worldview, but these actions result from the worldview, which was that the world was a place for them to go out and conquer.

Why did they have that worldview? Well I don't know. I haven't researched the Vikings, but you certainly can and take that and apply that attitude to one of your species. This is what's known as an analogue, which was touched upon earlier in this podcast. An analogue is when we take something from Earth and mold it to our fictional world.

The Europeans had a certain worldview when they were exploring the world and conquering places like what is now the United States. The Native Americans had a different world view. If we can't think of a group like this, then we can take a famous leader like Genghis Khan and research who he was and the people that he led and what their attitude was.

GOVERNMENT AND WORLD VIEW

The world view will also impact what sort of government the species typically has in their own settlements. Many of us don't find discussions of government interesting, but I promise you that if you read *Creating Places*, which is volume 2 in *The Art of World Building* book series, I will change this for you because I go into quite a bit of detail about the difference between one government type and another, at least at the high level, so that you can make a good decision about what to do in your world.

Monarchies, dictatorships, and republics are all vastly different in the outlook of the species who has created that form of government. This is not to say that one species will only have one of these. For example, humans have all of them. If you create elves, for example, or something similar, they might have a monarchy in one place and a dictatorship in another. Now we don't associate elves with having dictatorships, but anything is possible if you really want to be that way.

One of the things we want to avoid is having a monoculture where a species is their culture because they're all the same. This might seem like a contradiction I'm bringing up because I am talking about creating generalizations, but we can create more than one generalization.

When it comes to both worldview and society, we should decide whether they respect human rights, as we call them here on Earth. Do they believe in personal liberty? This is again going to inform the type of government that they invent. Do they believe in marriage? Do they accept divorce? What is their view on homosexuality? How do they feel about the accumulation of wealth? Is this something they look to or do they try to have the wealthy spread that money to the poor?

Do they believe that personal liberty is so prized that they don't have many laws and therefore there might be more crime? That could in turn lead to certain people finding their sentiments desirable because they're the kind of people who are up to something. By contrast, there might be goodhearted people who don't want to live in such a place because they don't want to feel like they don't have that kind of protection. This could also result in weapons being allowed to be carried openly or a policy could be there to prevent that sort of thing, where people have to lock up their guns or their swords before entering town.

Sometimes to get at the worldview, we have to think of some practical limitations and how those apply. This is arguably what we're really after because we don't want to be writing passages about the worldview. We want the worldview to inform the behavior that our characters can get away with. Restrictions that they would run afoul of are also important.

We should also consider how they raise their young. Do we have a nuclear family where there is usually a father and a mother, or is it more of an open-ended kind of thing where it's almost like animals where the child is born into society and for a few years it's attached to the mother, but then it's set free? This can have a huge impact on society.

All of this affects the customs, such as birth, death, and burial rituals and things like weddings and divorce. This can affect simple things like whether we shake hands, or hold doors for people, or salute people. Do people trade gifts upon meeting? While this is a custom, it may come out of the worldview of wishing happiness on people, for example. There are so many things that we could do with worldview that it can be overwhelming, and that's why there's a whole volume on culture in this series. We will touch on this much more later but I wanted to get you thinking about the general worldview of your species.

And one of the biggest questions to ask yourself is whether they are a force for good or evil? Are they part of the problem or part of the solution?

HUMAN COMMENTARY

The last thing I want to talk about here is human commentary. What do I mean? Well, one of the best uses for species is to offer a contrast to us. For example, if you think that humans are greedy in general, or that this is a failing of ours, then you can create a species who is very generous and craft a story where this conflict comes up.

I've read many stories where elves are either immortal or they live 1000 years or more, which of course is far in excess of humans. This has often been used to depict humans as being impatient. This is practically a cliché at this point, but you get the idea. This sort of comparison can make the audience relate to our work a little better. That really depends on our audience, but I think that even people in their teens enjoy reading something that makes them think a little bit while they're being entertained.

Part of what we're getting at here is the relationship of our species to everyone else. It's a good idea to decide how our species not only interacts with humans, but with each other, if we are creating more than one of them. It's a little too easy to just figure out how the humans interact with them and not think about the relationships with each other. But this is something to work on later after you've already got a pretty good idea of what the species is like. And what your second species is like.

In the free templates that you can download by joining the newsletter, I do have a section for working these out. As with everything, it's designed to get you thinking and is not mandatory. Nothing in world building is mandatory.

We should decide if the species are enemies or friends and why. And do they have any legendary battles or animosities? Maybe they have treaties. They might've been allies in the past but are enemies now. There should also be classic understandings or stereotypes that each has about the other. Humans may share some of these. Crafting all of this requires having a good understanding of worldview.

NOT COVERED

There are several other issues that we can discuss when it comes to inventing a species or race. One of those is what languages are spoken and whether they have their own written language. The ability to read or write is going to have a huge impact on how sophisticated the society can be. The subject is covered in more detail in *Creating Life*, but I'm not going to cover it here.

I'm also not going to cover creating a history for our species and how this can make it more diverse. An even bigger subject I'm not going to cover in this podcast is the supernatural, which is not only phenomena and magic, but their use of godly powers, such as the ability to channel a god's power through their own body. For those who read both fantasy and science fiction, we're also not going to cover the use of technology or combat. Both of these can be found in *Creating Life*.

WHERE TO START

My final words on how to create a species or race is to talk about where to start. The top-down approach means inventing a species at the high level and working our way into details. For example, we could decide on a sea dwelling species and then start working into details such as whether they have gills, or whether they can survive out of water, or even if they can walk on land.

The bottom-up approach means working on the details and then slowly integrating them into a unified whole. Maybe we first decide that the species has sharp claws, a barbed tail, and it carries people off at night but is seldom seen doing so, and it leaves no trace of where it went. From these details and more, maybe we decide that it's a sea dwelling creature and that the reason it's got claws is that these are for catching fish, and the reason people disappear is that they are taken underwater to a cave or maybe even just drowned. This big picture is suggested by the details that we thought of first.

Regardless of your approach, there's really no right or wrong way to do it and as mentioned before, we will crisscross back and forth on our species and other inventions, changing and updating things as we go along.

HOW TO CREATE WORLD FIGURES

H ello and welcome to *The Art of World Building Podcast*, episode number six. Today's topic is how to create world figures like heroes, villains, and more. This includes talking about what made them famous, their relationships and history, and what kind of cool gadgets they might have and why. This material and more is discussed in Chapter 4 of *Creating Life*, volume 1 in *The Art of World Building* book series.

HOW WILL WE USE THEM?

The advice in this episode applies equally well to heroes, villains, martyrs, celebrities, or any other public figures we might want to mention. Whether we invent them or not, every world is going to have its famous people. It can make our world seem more realistic if we have some of them for our characters to refer to. For example, a knight might look up to a famous knight who exemplified the values of the knighthood. A priest will do the same with their religion. There will always be famous pilots in science fiction. If our story takes place on the water, there will be famous pirates and other captains.

And of course, without villains, what's the point of writing a story? Some of our villains will be local to the story that we're telling, but some of them will be a much larger figure, someone who dominated the world or even multiple planets in science fiction.

Whether our characters are good or bad. They usually have someone that they look up to. That said, we don't usually need to go into a lot of detail about these characters. Just a line here or there can be used. In those moments where we do mention them, we usually want to mention why they are looked up to. For example, maybe there's a famous knight who changed the tide of war, maybe by sacrificing himself. In so doing, he might have restored the honor of the knighthood, if there was something wrong with it. If you're wondering where I'm getting this from, it's from the *Dragonlance* series.

In fantasy, we might also have a wizard who is responsible for people fearing wizards in general. Of course, wizards are very powerful so we don't necessarily need a reason for everyone to fear them, but sometimes we might want to have an especially bad person who had a big effect, where magic is now restricted in some way, for example.

We could also have an inspiring political or religious figure who is responsible for changing the way people think about various issues or human rights. The person I'm thinking of right now is Martin Luther King. Of course, if we base someone on him, we are doing an analogue, which was discussed in an earlier episode. This is once again a very useful technique for inventing things for our planet.

We could have a famous explorer whose ship vanished, or it could be their plane, such as with Amelia Earhart. This example also gives us a lost plane, ship, or spacecraft, which can eventually be found by other characters. We might have a dictator who was responsible for trying to exterminate a race, and this is especially useful in fantasy when we have more than just different varieties of humans, but we might have different versions of elves or dwarves, and somebody somewhere wants to exterminate some of them.

Even goodhearted people might decide that ogres or goblins might need to be wiped out so that they are no longer a threat, but even with just humans, we can still do this as we have done here on Earth, where Adolf Hitler and of course Nazi Germany tried to exterminate Jewish people. Other versions of this are a little bit less extreme but have happened more recently.

We could also have a warrior who is known for his skills but who ends up dying peacefully from something relatively innocuous like the flu. Who am I thinking of? Bruce Lee, the martial artist.

If we want to create a martyr for religion, we can just look up any number of them that have occurred over the course of human civilization here on Earth. And of course, there's the big one: Jesus Christ.

We might also want to include lowly figures like a bounty hunter or an assassin who killed an especially important person such as an emperor or a king. And of course, rulers or other famous people are good people to create, mostly because they are so well known and they often do things that have a huge impact on a large number of people. And even long after they are gone, their impact is often still felt. And if you're looking for inspiration for famous rulers, you just have to go back into our own history. People like Julius Caesar come to mind.

Generally, if you look at these figures, they have done something that has had a lasting impact and this is why we still know who they are thousands of years later.

WHY ARE THEY FAMOUS?

And that brings us to the important subject of why these people are famous. There are a few questions we can ask ourselves to help us envision this person that we're going to create. One of those is, what are we hoping to achieve? Do we want a character for people to admire or to fear?

Let's use the example of a hero. Maybe we have a character called Kier and he is a knight. He most likely has another knight that he looks up to and we'll call this knight Vallen. And the latter is a famous knight. We could decide that he is alive today and maybe Kier knows him. In this scenario, Kier is likely to mention him in his thoughts or even to others more than once. Vallen may even appear in the book. That makes Vallen a character we need to flesh out a little bit more.

On the other hand, if he is not going to be a character in the book, either because he lives on another continent or just far away, or he's long dead, we don't need to develop this character of Vallen that much. The reason is that we're not going to have many opportunities to mention Vallen. In most scenarios, I would probably only have Kier mention him once or maybe twice in an entire story, even if it's a novel.

I would probably have Kier mention him early on in the characterization of Kier, and then if there's a critical point in the story where Kier feels that he is not living up to the virtues of Vallen or which he stood for, then I might mention Vallen again. Otherwise, we're probably not going to have much use for this. If our use for Vallen is limited, then we only need a little bit of information about him, such as what he stands for. These virtues can be based on what we need for the character of Kier and for our story. Or if we are creating a historical figure for use in general on our world, then we can be a little bit more open-ended.

We can decide that Vallen has whatever character traits we think might be interesting and maybe the most useful for the most number of stories that we write on that world. If we can't decide on one set of character traits that Vallen could have over another, then why don't we just create two knights at different points in history? There's no reason we can't have this. What are the odds that there is only one famous knight? In fact, we might want to create more than one on purpose and have them represent different things so that some people tend to favor one versus the other, or maybe they think of one or the other in different circumstances. This exercise can be done whether we're talking about knights, assassins, villains, or whatever else.

Regardless of who, what we're talking about right now are the character traits that this person embodies. For a knight character, the morale is something that comes to mind. Morale is usually associated with a deed. For example, someone might have extraordinary morale, but unless they have the opportunity to demonstrate that, no one's ever going to know. We would probably want to have a situation where that character was facing overwhelming odds, for example, and they overcame them anyway, and they did so partly by standing their ground despite the low odds of victory.

On that note, they don't even have to have been victorious. Maybe they died for this. But, as a result of standing up like that, maybe they caused a delay in the opposing forces, or something else positive happened as a result of their sacrifice. And sacrifice also makes it clear that they are humble, in the sense that they are willing to lay down their life, but it also shows that they are willing to champion an idea to the point of sacrificing their life for that.

What we end up here is with a character who is moral and is therefore a moral compass for other characters to look up to, and this can be true whether that character is a knight or not. The result might be that Vallen is not a knight, but Kier looks up to him anyway because of what he stood for. This is a good way to create variety because it can seem a little bit too planned to have a knight worshiping a knight, and to have an assassin worshiping a famous assassin, and always having this sort of one-to-one relationship. Sometimes people might admire someone for some of the traits but not others.

A famous person might also be famous for their characteristics, such as their morality, but then at the end of their life, something unusual happens that seems to betray that, so there's a conflict for our other character who wants to look up to them. The point I'm making here is that we sometimes idealize a hero, and at the same time vilify a villain, to the point that we say that there exclusively one way or another way.

This touches back to something that I spoke about in the previous episode, about simplifying things to good versus evil. There's a tendency for most of us to do this. If that sort of simplicity works for your story, then go ahead, but if you're looking for something that's a little bit more varied, then try to give your hero some warts, and try to give your villain some positive things that they may have done.

For example, a villain might have sacrificed themselves at the end of their life for some noble cause, and this could've been a change of heart or something else. It's something that makes them a little bit more realistic. The only potential problem with doing such a thing is that we have to make up a reason for this. You have to decide if it's really worth it for the character. Again, if our story is only going to have us mentioning that person once or twice, then maybe we don't want to do something more complex like that. On the other hand, if we're writing a longer story like a trilogy or more, and we're going to use the world longer, then we might want to go ahead and create these more complex characters.

Now I do think that all characters actually are more complex. The question is whether we want to portray them that way or not.

More Reasons to be Famous

Our world figure could be famous for their character, but they could also be famous for their deeds. When we do this, we are also creating history, which is a subject that we will touch upon repeatedly throughout this podcast. This can work either way. We can try to create a world figure, which results in history, or we can be trying to create history, which results in a world figure. What I would recommend is that you have a dedicated history file on your computer, and that you also have a dedicated file for each one of your world figures, or have all of them in one file.

What you will end up doing is working in both files, so let's say that we're working on your world figure, and are trying to think of an event that made that person famous. What we want to write down for that figure in their file is their role in that event, but when it comes to the larger event and what was going on, like let's say it was a war and this person was involved in the end of it, that should probably be described a little bit more in the history file.

What we're trying to do is minimize the redundancy a little bit. By having both files open at the same time, it's relatively easy to just keep going back and forth between them and writing information in one or the other based on what we're writing. I frequently do this and find myself writing too much about that war when I'm in the world figure's file, but then I can move it into the history file. One reason we might want to do this is that when we are creating this history, we might want to create more than one world figure.

Let's take a moment and talk about how I would write an entry in that world history file. In the history file, the only thing I would say about the character is something very brief, such as, "Lord Vallen did so-and-so at the final battle and the result was the end of the war and. As a result, this, that, or the other thing happened." I wouldn't describe this character in the history file. I may or may not want to leave a note to myself to look into the world figure's file, but most likely I will already know that I've got one of these and there are various people who are fleshed out a little bit more in the file.

As for what goes into the world figure's file, let's talk about that. We're going to talk about the reason they're famous and the facts surrounding that. One point to make there is that there could be facts and then there could be rumors. They might be famous for something that didn't even actually happen, or which didn't happen in the way that people think it happened. If we're going to create that kind of detail, it's something that we should only do if we are intending to reveal that to our characters in particular, and have our characters become disillusioned when they find out that something is very different. This can shake someone's faith in a cherished world figure.

We're also going to write down this characters traits or status, such as whether they are dead or alive, what kind of possessions they have, their family members, and their relationships with other species. We're also going to want to talk about their history, which includes their origins and their demise if they are dead. And then of course some of what happened in between.

We might also want to talk about their training and skills, because that might also have made them famous, and then of course their deeds. You don't have to remember everything I just said because there is a handy appendix. It's number three from the *Creating Life* book, and you can just download this by joining the newsletter. It's a handy fill in the blanks form that will help you to think about all of these things, and it provides not only the space for you to write down these things, but it provides some commentary on the things you might want to think about, including what is being mentioned in this episode. And all of the things I just mentioned are the other topics we're going to talk about today.

WHAT IS THEIR STATUS?

We touched on this earlier, but we should decide whether our character is dead or alive. Let's say that they died. Are they really dead or just presumed so? How did they die, and was that a satisfying conclusion for their life for either the audience or the characters involved in the stories? They might just be missing and incorrectly identified as dead. They might've even faked their death.

All of these options add some interesting depth to what we've done, but that's exactly why a lot of people have already done this kind of thing, especially in TV and film. My advice would be to do this sort of thing sparingly.

If the character really is dead, decide how they died. Was it in battle, or something else extraordinary, or was it a peaceful and? They might've gone on to become a ruler and end up in a famous tomb somewhere. That can be true whether they became a ruler or not.

That brings up another question: where are they buried? Are they buried somewhere out of the way where no one can get to that grave for some reason? Maybe because they're very dangerous still, even in death? Maybe because they have a valuable item that was buried with them. Or they might be buried in a public cemetery where people can come and pay their respects. This might even result in a kind of pilgrimage that a knight character might do, for example, to pay homage to that knight. It might even be expected or required of them. This could result in a pilgrimage for our character Kier, who went to visit the grave of Lord Vallen at some point in his mid-20s, and maybe even met one of the characters who is also in the current storyline we're telling, while he's on that pilgrimage. This doesn't necessarily mean that the other character was also on that pilgrimage, because we meet all kinds of people when we travel, regardless of the reason. This is one way to work this into narration or dialogue.

What about if the character is still alive? Are they at the height of the powers? That would be true if the thing that made them famous was recent, as in the last 5 or 10 years. Maybe they are still around and doing good or bad things to people. Or maybe this was 50 years ago and now they are retired somewhere in old age, and comfortably living by the sea or something.

This brings up another question and that is whether this character is okay with their fame or if they are hiding from it? Imagine today where we have these paparazzi who never leave anybody alone and the tabloids, where they keep following people long after their fame has ended. We get these "where are they now?" kind of stories. This is the sort of thing that's probably going to happen in a more futuristic society like ours or even in sci-fi, but in a fantasy setting, it's more likely that the character's going to be able to retire to a quiet life without people pestering them all the time. But there might be some people who still seek them out. Are they okay with this or do they just want to be left alone?

What if it's only been 20 years since they did the famous deeds? If they're a warrior, then some people would probably say that they're past their prime. Does this person like hearing that or do they get offended?

Yet another option for us is for this character to be imprisoned. Obviously, this is more likely if they are a villain, but there's no reason that a hero can't also be in be imprisoned in a place that is not kind to the values for which he stood. One question for all of our characters is whether their imprisonment is known or not. Even if we decide that the average person has no idea, it's always best if there are few people who know the truth, and those people want to do something about it, such as rescuing that character.

There's a lot of fun to be had in saying that most people don't know a certain thing, or most people know something and are basically wrong, and a select group of characters, obviously the ones that we're writing with, are the ones who know the truth. And they're going to do something about it. What this allows us to do in a world we're going to use repeatedly and for a long time is to say things are one way many times, and then in a subsequent story, we talk about the truth. We just have to be careful about this and not contradict ourselves too much.

There is a trick for this and it's one that I use myself. I always have a character be the one who says something when that thing is not really true. They believe it's true when they say it, but that means that me as an author, I am not lying. I did not say it in narration. If I say "Vallen is dead" in narration, and then I later decide he's not, I'm the one who lied. If a character says it, and then they turn out to be wrong, well, that happens to us all the time in real life anyway. You could say that this is a cheat on my part, but it's perfectly valid.

If we don't want to do that, we can say narration that "everyone thinks Lord Vallen is dead," but the problem is if we say "everyone thinks," we're basically dropping a hint that maybe everyone's wrong and therefore it won't come as a surprise if Lord Vallen turns out to not be dead. We may want to do that on purpose to create ambiguity, but we might not want to.

WHAT GADGETS DO THEY HAVE?

Everyone likes cool stuff, so let's talk about the possessions that our world figure might have. This is a subject not to go overboard with and what I mean is that we should only give our character one or maybe two items that are especially cool. Otherwise, the law of diminishing returns kicks in. What I mean by that is that the coolness of each of the items goes down the more items we give them. Besides, we arguably want them to have one especially cool item. This is the one that might be associated with them, like Thor's hammer. I would say the name of that hammer but it's impossible to pronounce, and some of you are probably going to laugh about that.

But that does bring up another point that sometimes we want to name these items. There's a long tradition of this such as the name Stormbringer being the blade that Elric of Melnibone wielded. And as a side for those of you who are following my fiction and got my free book, *The Ever Fiend*, by joining my fiction newsletter, yes I did steal the name Stormbringer for my character Talon Stormbringer.

We're trying to decide on is what item to give our character. The obvious way to get going with this is to think of something that has something to do with what they are famous for. For example, knights are famous for their armor and swords. We might want to give them a famous sword or armor. They might also have a horse that was particularly large, fearsome, or followed their commands or was particularly loyal to them, or which simply survived through a great number of adventures that they went on. A famous horse or steed is certainly one option we can do if we are looking for more than one thing. In this case, you can have the famous horse and sword.

In science fiction it might be a spaceship like the Millennium Falcon in *Star Wars*. Or it might be a laser gun. It depends what kind of gun you're going to use.

The trick to these weapons is to make them distinctive in some way. And the best bet there is to make it capable of doing something that most similar weapons are not capable of doing. For example, let's say you got a laser gun that eventually runs out of charge or does so relatively quickly. Your character could have one that never does so. However, as cool features go, this one is not that exciting. Well, what if this one shoots around corners? Well, that's a little bit ridiculous, but you get the idea. You want to do something unique with this item.

The example of Thor's hammer is a weapon that can be thrown and returned to its owner. It is also so heavy that no one else can lift it. That brings to mind Excalibur, the sword that no one could pull out of the rock. This brings up another point that these items can be famous because of how they were acquired. That could be one of the reasons anyway. Some of you may remember that in the *Star Wars* universe, the Millennium Falcon was given to Han Solo during a bet that he won. However, that is just an interesting tidbit. It's not the reason that it's famous. It's mostly that it's associated with Harrison Ford's character.

This brings up another point that this ship is one that's known for its ricketiness. It has its issues. They have to kick it. They've got a do things to it to make it work the way it's supposed to. It's a beloved ship but it's got its problems and this is one way to make it famous for our characters because it acquires personality through flaws.

This leads to an important distinction however. This particular ship is not really famous in the *Star Wars* universe so much as it is famous here on Earth. This is a subtle difference. The ship also brings up the idea of a broken item. One thing I'm thinking of here is of a sword that has been broken. In *The Lord of the Rings*, there's a famous sword that has been broken and eventually becomes whole again. This is a momentous event.

In science fiction, we could have a weapon that is no longer powered for whatever reason, and the power source is something that's rare for is assumed gone, and we might have a storyline where someone tries to recover this weapon and make it work again.

Earlier we talked about a character still being alive or possibly being imprisoned, or even being dead. In all cases, the question remains: what happens to their famous items? If they are buried with it, that could explain why they are buried in an out-of-the-way place. Do people seek them out in an effort to take that item and use it for their own purposes? Did the famous character know that this was a possibility and have they taken steps to safeguard this item? Did they give it to a younger person who is now the one going out and doing things? Do they spread a rumor that it is broken or lost? We have lots of options for creating an interesting item for our character.

THEIR RELATIONSHIPS

Our final subject for today will be about the world figure's relationships. This is another way to make them much more interesting. However, it is once again something to do only if we think we will use the setting more often and have the opportunity to mention these details. The kinds of relationship that we can create are the typical ones for everyone: parents, siblings, lovers, and children. There's also the entire extended family. But we really don't want to go into that kind of detail in most cases.

Something to consider is whether the world figure and the family are basically of the same disposition about things. Using the oversimplification of good versus evil, if we're creating a villain, well, is the whole family evil, or is this person the black sheep? By contrast, if the character is a hero, is the rest of the family okay with that or do they have problems with the status this person has acquired? Do they have more traditional resentments that family might have out of jealousy? Is the entire family prone to heroism?

In most cases, we're not going to want to go with yes. In other words, we're not going to want to have a hero character who has a heroic family, and a villain character who comes from an evil family. It's just too simple. And it doesn't really matter what kind of family we're talking about, whether those are the parents or the children, the question is still going to come up: what do the family members think of this character?

What we're really after here is whether family is proud of them or ashamed of them. If there ashamed, and they're all sharing the last name, and that last name is distinctive like Skywalker, for example, then do they change their name? Do they try to live anonymously? Do they try to disavow this person and just not be associated with them?

Are they mad that this person brings shame on their name or that they are experiencing guilt by association?

By contrast, if the character was a hero and went around destroying all sorts of bad guys, well then are those bad guys or their relatives or henchmen trying to get back at that hero? And if they can't find the hero, do they decide to go after family members instead? This is especially attractive if that hero is no longer around but revenge is still desired. If you can't take it out on the hero because they are dead and desecrating the corpses isn't enough, for example, then maybe you go after the family members.

This might result in a family going into hiding. The family might also have powerful friends if that hero had powerful friends who are now taking care of the family as a result of this. This could cause another heroic character who was friends with that hero to feel an obligation to protect his fallen friend's family.

We were talking earlier about having a main character like our knight Kier referencing a long dead character like Lord Vallen. Well, what if Lord Vallen was a relative who is now long gone? It could have been several generations earlier. Kier might be expected to live up to that example and not appreciate this. He might feel pressure. He might not even want to be a knight but is forced into this.

Another thing we should keep in mind is what this character's relationship was like with different species. He might've been a hero to the elves but a villain to the dwarves. This will go back to the events that made this character famous. Or at least, that's one way of going about creating this sort of dynamic. Did this character save the elves but in doing so, doomed the dwarves? Traditionally, we see elves and dwarves as mostly being on the same side of conflicts, so it might be that the elves and dwarves thinks he's a hero, and many humans do, but that the goblins and ogres of the world do not. This is a little bit more obvious and is probably even expected, which is why we might want to do something a little more interesting.

THEIR ORIGINS

We've already talked about their demise, so let's talk a little bit about their origins. It can sometimes help to have decided that the character is from another continent, or on other planets in science fiction. This might give them a set of characteristics or behaviors that are markedly different from the place where they became famous. This might even be part of why they're famous. This can also apply to their appearance. For example, if everyone is raven-haired and has brown eyes, but this character is from a place where people were blonde and blue-eyed, then this appearance might be one of the reasons they are famous.

If we decided that they are from far away, we should figure out why they came to where they became famous. We don't need an elaborate reason because in SF and fantasy, we often have characters who are traveling for adventure or something a little more intelligent than just saying they wanted some big adventure. They may have been driven out, or they may be seeking a better life.

Something that I talk about in the book but that I'm not going to cover in this podcast is the training this person might have received, and the skills that they could've picked up either in that training or along the way. This is one way to justify the abilities they have and which are on display. In the book, I also give guidance on where to start. Creating world figures can add an interesting element to our world and is something that you can do at any time.

Join the newsletter and templates to get started.

HOW TO CREATE MONSTERS

Hello and welcome to The Art of World *Building Podcast*, episode number seven. Today's topic is how to create monsters. This includes talking about how they differ from animals and species, how to make their origins interesting, their motivation, and more. This material and more is discussed in Chapter 5 of *Creating Life*, volume 1 in *The Art of World Building* book series.

DEFINING MONSTER

We all know what a monster is, but we might also be creating a species or animals, so let's try to be clear about the differences. The term implies something harmful, unnatural, or morally objectionable, whether that's a physical deformity or psychological one. Storytellers have created monsters to get across one of those ideas, usually as a warning. In other words, traditionally monsters weren't there simply to be killed by our heroes, although this is something we often see in science fiction and fantasy. The storytellers of old usually approached it that way, but in our modern times, it seems that people often create monsters just to have something for our heroes to kill.

While there's nothing wrong with that, it suggests that there are two kinds of monsters: those that have nothing interesting about them other than being scary, and those that are representative of some evil. It's arguably harder to create the latter, which is probably why a lot of modern storytellers don't bother. While this is fine, be aware that you could do more with your monster if you have a mind to create something that is morally objectionable.

We can do that by having the monster represents something. And it should be an issue that has something to do with either the story or the characters. For example, maybe your monster is a fallen knight who has been transformed into something hideous, and that the reason this happened to him is that he somehow failed in his moral duty as a knight, and this is the punishment. By punishment, I don't necessarily mean that someone forced this person to become this way, but maybe their morally bankrupt choices led them to do something and exposed them to something dangerous, and that phenomenon turned him into a monster. In this way, we can imply that their character and their faults led them to become a monster. And if we're not looking for that sort of commentary, then we don't need to do this.

Another angle we might want to explore is that sometimes a monster is thought to foreshadow some sort of evil happening. This can be one reason why they are cast out of society. As long as they are around, people might be worried about this event taking place. An example of this would be someone who is born with a birth defect that makes them physically hideous to other people, and that causes people to not only decide that they are a monster physically, but maybe morally they represent something terrible. The arrival of a person with this moral flaw could herald the end of civilization, for example. That's kind of extreme, but it could be also just the fall of some kind of idea, or some idea has been tarnished by the arrival of this morally objectionable person.

Something we're alluding to here is the unfortunate reality that at least humans tend to judge other people based on physical characteristics. We will decide that someone attractive is good and someone unattractive is bad. Psychologists have actually done studies proving that people do indeed do this, where good appearances is associated with good character. This is an unfortunate reality that we all have to live with.

However, we could have a species of our invention, or even the standard ones, that don't act like this. They might be the ones who take in a monster, or a person who is considered a monster, who has been cast out by another society. They may become known for becoming a refuge for monsters. What if you have a character who, at the end of a book, becomes a monster for the next book, and then goes to those people for refuge? It's an interesting arc.

We might also have a species or race, or even animal, who is initially considered to be a monster by space traveling characters who are unfamiliar with this life form. We'll touch upon this more in a few minutes, but the question of numbers is one of the ones we should consider, because typically a monster is considered to be a one off. There's only one of them, not ten or a thousand.

We could have a scenario where the space travelers encounter just one of them and think it's a monster, and then in time they find out it's not. It's an animal or species.

This brings up another subject, and that is the word "sentient." The definition of this word is the ability to sense, feel, and experience, which means that any animal is technically sentient. But in science fiction and fantasy, the word is often used to imply that someone or something either does or does not have humanlike mental capabilities. This isn't really what the word means, but you're probably familiar with that, if you've heard of it at all, so we're going to go ahead with that understanding of what the word sentient means throughout this episode.

MONSTERS VERSUS SPECIES

Let's talk about the difference between a monster and a species. The main difference is arguably the mind. We don't expect a monster to have a philosophy, culture, or a society. In fact, there's usually only one of them, and we think of these issues as things that distinguish humans from animals. Monsters are often considered to be much closer to animals than humans. I said humans here, but in the context of fantasy and science fiction, that includes any of the so-called sentient races like elves and dwarves.

A monster isn't going to have its own language either, because if there's only one of them, it doesn't need to develop a language at all, not to mention one to communicate with others of its kind when they don't exist. If it can speak at all, it's going to be one of the languages of another species. The lack of others is also why it's not going to have a society or culture, because that implies that there's more than one of them.

While the mind of the monster is typically considered quite limited compared to those of humans, there's no reason we can't have an intelligent monster. Dracula is one that comes to mind, but he was once a human. This is where his intelligence originates and it has not been dramatically reduced by having become what we consider to be a monster. Whatever transformation he underwent did not cause the problem.

But that's not to say that we can't have that be the case. Zombies come to mind as something that's typically very stupid, and then when we have one that is slightly more intelligent, we consider that an aberration.

Monsters are typically unsophisticated and are much like an animal that is essentially backed into a corner and wants to eat us for dinner or because we came into their territory. We don't imagine that they are sitting around writing symphonies or great literature. In theory they wouldn't be able to appreciate these either, but anyone can enjoy music.

And then of course you have the example of Dr. Frankenstein's monster, which actually became educated enough to read a book. If you've never read *Frankenstein*, Mary Shelley has all of these passages in there where the monster is thinking a lot about its place in the world, what it is doing here, and how did it get abandoned by its creator. It's a relatively sophisticated monster in the sense that it can actually read and understand philosophy, but most of us don't know that because Hollywood tends to take Frankenstein's monster and turn it into something that's walking around moaning and groaning, and trying to kill people, of course.

This philosophy-minded monster is the exception rather than the rule. While we are generalizing here, we're trying to get a baseline understanding of what we mean by "monster." While we might all know what that means, sometimes thinking about these things can make us think of exceptions that we can do for variety.

MONSTERS VS. ANIMALS

Let's also talk about monsters versus animals and what the differences are. I mentioned this earlier, but I think the single biggest difference is numbers. There's a reason there is only one type of each monster, and that is because that it implies they are abnormal, which means that they are not common. Once we have dozens, hundreds, or thousands of them, they become common and they are not abnormal and therefore they are not a monster anymore.

This immediately reminds me of zombies. They are considered monsters but that's not the word we use to describe them most of the time. We refer to them as zombies. Maybe this is a technicality, but once we have more than one of them, we don't use "monster" to describe them. We instead have a name for the whole group of them, such as "zombies." Zombies are certainly monstrous, but we don't call them "monsters."

Think of it this way: if you and I were standing together, and a dozen zombies were coming toward us, and I said, "Oh look, it's a bunch of monsters," he would say, "No it's not. They're zombies." In other words, "zombie" is more specific than "monster."

And one of the things implied by that specific word "zombie," is that zombies have predictable character traits. How do we know that they're predictable? Because there's more than one of them. By contrast, a monster is unique and therefore we don't know what it can do unless we have experience with it or we've heard about it. You could almost say that monster is a fallback term if we don't know what else to refer to it by.

Assuming for the sake of argument that zombies are real, the first person to run across just one of them would've probably thought that it was a monster, but once they discovered that there were more of them, and that they had shared traits, they probably would've come up with a name, and that name would be "zombie."

None of this means we can't have two identical monsters. That might contradict everything I just said, but what if one event created more than one of them? Let's say that you have a human who was exposed to radiation, or in this case, two humans. Would that radiation cause the same mutation in both of them? There's no way to know. I'm not a geneticist, so I can't do more than speculate, but it's certainly reasonable to conclude that it might cause two different mutations, resulting in two different monsters.

But let's say there are two monsters that are identical, and they can reproduce. Once they do so, they start to move away from being monsters toward being animals. Either that, or if they all have a certain amount of intelligence, they might start becoming a species. Why? Because they're going to start developing their own language, society, philosophy, and all that other stuff. What this means is that we could have something that starts off as a monster, but then it evolves into something greater than that.

As world builders, we have license to do whatever we want, but at least this thought exercise gets you thinking about what you're doing.

Origins – Accidental Monsters

We've touched on their origins a little bit, but let's focus on this more. We don't need to tell the audience where the monster originated, but this can make them more interesting. The first question is whether they exist on purpose or by accident. Let's talk about accidental monsters first.

In science fiction and fantasy, it's really easy to have a character come in contact with an advanced technology, an unexplained phenomenon, or magic that turns them into a monster. Many of our comic book characters come from such things. We don't even need to explain the sort of thing because people already accept it. We just say that someone ran into this and now they're a monster, and that's all there is to it.

One thing we should is consider whether that phenomenon, or whatever caused it, is still around and is capable of producing more monsters, whether those are the same or different. If the phenomenon was short-lived, such as something like an explosion, there's probably not going to be a recurrence of this. On the other hand, if the phenomenon is one that's perpetually located where it is, then it could produce more of them, unless we decide that it's in a remote place, or that people realize that it can do this and now there's some sort of protection around it, so that people can't get there. If the source is perpetual, but we don't want to have hundreds of these monsters, then this is one way of going around that. It also gives us the option to change our mind later and have another person become this sort of monster, or a different variety.

Typically, if we have an accident that results in a monster, that accident happened to a living entity, such as a person or an animal. If an accident affected something inanimate like a broom, we don't consider the result to be a monster. In this case, I'm thinking of *The Sorcerer's Apprentice*, where the broom is doing its own thing. Do we think of that as a monster? No. We think of it as an animated object. But there's no reason we couldn't give it more features to make it more like a monster. And what would that features be? Sentience: the ability to think, sense, and experience. For the most part, an animated object like a broom does not have that.

I say that because we could decide that it does, then we've created a monster, and we're using sentience to distinguish between an animate object and a monster.

What about plants? These are living matter. Could we have a plant that becomes a monster? Sure, why not? The accident could have given the plant increased sentience. The big problem with having a plant as a monster is that plants are typically rooted to the spot. Something that can't chase after you is not particularly disturbing. All you have to do is stand far enough away.

But what if we gave that plant the ability to lure people closer, such as hypnotism or some sort of pheromone that makes them come closer? Now it's starting to become a monster. The plant might also acquire the ability to cause hallucinations so that people don't realize its true nature. Maybe it causes someone to enter into a dreamlike state where they imagine that they are walking into their home, and laying down to sleep in their bed, when they are really lying down in the part of the plant that consumes living matter, like them.

But let's say that it was a human that became a monster, or one of our species. If this person is now a monster and has been in that state for decades, this might have rendered their original intelligence relatively muted so that they are now dumber than they used to be. This is one way to justify the monster's intelligence. Or we can simply decide that this dumbing down of them was instantaneous. Or they could be so horrified by what has happened to them, psychologically, that they've had the equivalent of a mental breakdown and they're just not in their right head about it. Would you blame them? I would probably lose my mind if I became a monster.

If something like an explosion caused our monster to exist, we might want to consider who caused that incident to happen. Why would we care about this? Well, for one, it gives us a little bit more back story and an incident in the history, but it also might give our monster something they might want to take revenge upon if it can remember. In a perfect world, the monster might decide to be forgiving, but where's the fun in that? Isn't it more interesting if the monster has an issue with someone and wants to go and find that person and destroy them or their family? Or even the society that it used to be part of and is now cast out of? Because it might not just be an individual who was responsible for the accident, but the society or parts of it.

And the monster could actually be the one who caused that accident themselves. Humans in particular have a tendency to not take responsibility for things that we do to ourselves, especially if it's really bad. It might just blame other people for this and still have a revenge issue.

ORIGINS – MONSTERS BY DESIGN

Let's talk about monsters that were created on purpose. Now by "on purpose" I don't mean something like Dr. Frankenstein, who was trying to create life and inadvertently created a monster. That is still an accident, though not in the sense of something exploding, for example. What we're really talking about is someone who wants to create a monster and has that intention from the outset.

A good question is why would someone do this? And the answer could be that the monster has a purpose. Maybe this monster is designed to guard something. Since there's only one of them, because monsters are, by definition, uncommon, then maybe no one knows what to expect or how to defeat this monster. Maybe the monster is designed to go around terrorizing a village because some sort of wizard wants this to be done. Maybe that wizard has a beef with that village and wants to freak everyone out. The monster could also just be a diversion while the wizard is going off and doing something else.

But what about the monster? Does it like having this purpose? Does it enjoy doing what it's doing? And is it bound to its creator somehow so that if something happens to that creator, the monster also suffers a bad fate? What if the creator dies and the monster is now on its own and is just going about trying to find its way? It might've just had a purpose and now doesn't other than just to survive. Maybe the monster is so loyal that it wants to take revenge on those who destroyed its master. The monster could've been harsh because the way its master treated it, and now that the master is gone, it might be a little bit more subdued and calmer, and less of a monster to people. Of course, if it already went around terrorizing people, no one's going to care that it's calmer now.

If the monster had a purpose, the purpose could've been achieved a long time ago, leaving it aimless. Such a monster is likely to be a little bit less dramatic than one that is still caught up in whatever purpose it has. Any monster that has been created on purpose is arguably more likely to be content with being a monster than someone who was turned into one.

While humans and other species have a moral and ethical code, a monster is portrayed as not having one, or as having one that is just radically different from ours, so that it appears like it doesn't have one. What I'm getting at here is that it's possible for the creator to happen imbued that monster with certain attitudes, such as protection of the creator or an item. Keeping this in mind while inventing such a monster will help you determine how it acts.

It can help if you know who created it and why. On that note, who would create a monster on purpose? We're probably thinking of wizards, gods, and maybe a mad scientist, like Dr. Frankenstein or Dr. Jekyll. We might also have our villain character who wants to purposely expose the hero character to some sort of phenomenon, either to kill them or to just destroy them in some other way, but the side effect is that it actually turned him into a monster. This villain may or may not know what is about to happen to this character, so this could either be an accident or a purposeful creation of a monster. The difference doesn't matter much.

The other source of monsters is evolution, such as in the *X-Men* series. The X-Men think of themselves as mutants, but some of the humans in the stories consider them monsters. This sets up a nice clash.

HABITAT

Let's talk a little bit about habitat, as where the monster lives is important to any story involving them, even if that home is never shown. The biggest reason we'll show the home is that our characters have stumbled upon it or purposely sought it out in order to destroy the monster. Once we do show this home, this gives us a lot of opportunities to characterize the monster itself through the home.

There could be any number of things that are lying around in this lair, including treasure, weapons, and the remains of victims. Those victims could either be animals or the species. In both cases, but especially in the case of species, the monster could've been defending itself, or it could have either lured those people there or gone out to kidnap them, bring them back, and then consume them to some degree.

As for why the remains are still there, it's possible that the monster is warning anyone else who stumbles upon this lair, or purposely goes seeking it out, that this is what's going to happen to them if they come in. It's also quite possible that the monster doesn't understand that disease can spread, or it might actually be immune to any such diseases. Another issue that could result from this, and again the monster might not care, is that the smell could actually lure other creatures in there or the species, who are realizing there's something dead over that way and they should check it out. They end up finding the lair, so the monster may or may not want to avoid this.

Of course, it's possible that our monster doesn't have a lair. This is a little bit uncommon because in literature, the stories are typically cautionary, meaning that the monster is living somewhere near a settlement that is supposed to learn a lesson from the monster's existence. A monster that goes away for a long period of time might prevent a population from learning that lesson.

On the other hand, there's no reason we can't have a monster that does like to travel. Maybe it does so seasonally, having more than one lair that it arrives at at different times of the year. This makes me think of migrating animals, but animals mostly do this for mating reasons. However, they also do it for food reasons, and their food may move around. A monster may be dining on people, so if the population doesn't travel, the monster probably doesn't. But what if you have a migratory species? You may end up with a monster that travels.

In worlds with magic or technology, there's no reason we can't have a monster who has acquired some other ability to get around. One of their victims might've had a magic ring that allows them to teleport. There might happen to be a magic portal somewhere near their lair, or they can at least get to it with relative ease, and maybe no one even knows that this is there, but that's how this monster is getting around. As you might imagine, this could make that monster significantly harder to track.

In some worlds, there's a kind of alternate reality that exists parallel to the normal one and where travel can happen at faster speeds, and maybe that land is where the monster exists. Or the monster just has access to that land and can get from one place to another in much faster time frames. I used that idea myself in my book *The Ever Fiend*. You can download that for free when you're joining *The Art of World Building* newsletter by checking the fiction checkbox. Is the Ever Fiend a monster? You'll have to read the book to find out if there's more than one of them.

In SF, we have another option for getting our monster from one place to another relatively quickly, and that would be technology. Now magic in fantasy, and technology in science fiction, are pretty much the same thing. It's just that one of them has an explanation in a technical way and the other one doesn't. But the more interesting option here is the ability to use something like a spaceship.

We don't normally think of a monster as having the mental capability to utilize a spaceship, but there's no reason it can't. In fact, the ship could be something that is relatively easy to control and it might even have something like autopilot. You just need to give your monster enough capability to command the ship and then you're good to go, and this is a little bit easier if your monster has some ability to speak, or it has a telepathic ability and there is a ship's artificial intelligence that can then do all the dirty work for the monster.

This ship could essentially function as a home away from home. How does the monster acquire such a ship? That's easy. The ship landed, and the monster killed the crew, and then it went on the ship and away it goes.

Let's talk a little bit more about a lair that's in a fixed location because there's another point we want to bring up here, and that point is that usually monsters don't want anyone to find that lair. The question remains: what do they do to prevent people from finding that lair? Does it go out of its way to avoid leaving tracks? Does it avoid leaving bodies? Does it purposely leave a trail but that trail is a trap? There might be magical or technological devices that allow people to track the monster more easily, so does the monster have the ability to thwart those devices?

WHAT DOES YOUR MONSTER WANT?

The last thing we're going to talk about today is the monster's motivation. What does it want?

Being left alone is a viable option. After all, if everyone thinks you're a monster, you probably don't want to be around them. In our modern world, with so much concern about bullying, we could decide that the monster simply doesn't want to be on the receiving end of this. In fact, you could say that this is emotionally abusive. It seems kind of silly to say that about a monster, because we consider them evil, and they're going around attacking people.

But certainly in modern children's stories we have stories where a monster is considered to be a misunderstood creature of some kind, and it's actually a nice guy. It's being bullied and therefore lashing out. This is a cliché, but the idea still stands: maybe the monster just wants to be left alone and not have to deal with this. This is arguably more likely if that monster was once a species of ours and has been turned into a monster, and he remembers enough of his old life that he doesn't want to experience this.

On that note, some of our species might think that the monster has the right to be left alone, provided it's not going around killing people. In our modern times, we have a lot of this "right to life" kind of thing going on, so are there people or species who think that our monster has a right to live?

Another motivation is hoarding treasure, but this is one that I've always had a problem with for one simple reason: if you're a monster and you're shunned by society, then treasure isn't going to do you any good. It's not like you can just waltz into town and say that you want to buy some item for 50 gold pieces, and the shop owner says that he will sell it to you for 60 instead. It's not going to happen. You're not going to have any bartering. This is money. The monster doesn't have any use for this.

Now the alternative to that is for the monster to think it's shiny, pretty, and the monster is kind of dumb, and it just likes this stuff. In this case, sure, hoarding treasure make sense. A better justification for treasure being around is that anyone who went there to try to kill the monster has ended up dead and their possessions are just lying around, casually discarded and the monster doesn't care or know what to do with it, so it's still just sitting there. That makes a lot more sense.

If the monster was never part of society, it's probably never going to understand the value of these things, unless of course it's a good observer and sees people coming into the lair trying to walk off with something especially shiny. It might reasonably conclude that it must be valuable, but is it even going to care that it is?

Another justification for treasure is that it does attract people, and if the monster wants to eat those people, then it makes sense to leave that treasure around.

What about food, since we were just talking about that? Everyone needs to eat and your monster is likely no exception. The bigger the monster, the more it's going to need to eat. The more frightening our monster is, the more likely we are to have it eating the species instead of the local cow population. Granted, it's not like people are not going to be upset about the livestock being eaten, because it's someone's likelihood, but it's much more horrifying and upsetting when people are being eaten. We might want to consider this as a motivation, that the monster is eating people just because it's hungry.

If the monster is a little bit smarter and more psychologically aggressive, maybe it's eating people just to freak them out. The problem with doing that is that of course people are going to get upset and probably going to come after me and try to kill me, so do I really want to do that? Maybe if I eat people once in a while, people will leave me alone, but if I eat people all the time, they're probably going to come after me.

If I eat people and I don't make it obvious that I'm the one who did it, then they're going to be less likely to pin it on me and come after me. This is one reason why I might kidnap someone and take them back to my lair and consume them there. It might also be smart for me to not leave the remains inside the opening of my cave, for example. Monsters may not be sophisticated enough to understand the difference between eating an animal and a person, so this is another option.

Another motivation that we just touched upon is security. No one likes to feel threatened and that includes monsters. This could be one of the reasons why they attack. This is especially true if it feels that people are encroaching on its territory. Maybe it's been living out in the wilderness for 50 years but that modern civilization is starting to chop down trees and other things, and slowly encroach, and the next thing you know, it starts attacking people.

We might not think that a monster would be afraid of anything, but even the apex predators in the world, like a shark, they are afraid of something. They cautiously approach food, and if that food is acting in such a way as to be unpredictable, or not a sure kill, something like a shark will actually go away.

In stories, we typically show monsters being largely unafraid of people, even when they are fully armored and have incredible weapons or prowess using them. They're going at it with this monster, but still the monster is coming on. This is one way in which a monster is different from an animal. A monster is typically more aggressive and ferocious. It doesn't back down as easily.

Another motivation we talked about earlier is revenge. I'm not to touch upon it again here, though it is covered a little bit more in the book. Another subject we aren't going to talk about in the podcast is the characteristics of our monster, such as its physical appearance and its skills, and how to make these more interesting and relevant for our audience. As always, the chapter concludes with a section on where to start.

HOW AND WHEN TO CREATE PLANTS

Hello and welcome to *The Art of World Building Podcast*, episode number eight. Today's topic is how to create plants. This includes talking whether you should do it at all, how to classify them, and what uses we can put them to. This material and more is discussed in Chapter 6 of *Creating Life*, volume 1 in *The Art of World Building* book series.

SHOULD WE CREATE THEM?

The first question we should ask ourselves is whether or not we should create plants. One great thing about plants is that it's much easier to do this than something like a species or a god. Even countries, governments, and other stuff about creating a place is significantly more involved than creating a plant. Even though it's so easy to create plants, this is one of the most optional things in world building, because if your world is anything at all like Earth, people are not even going to question it if you refer to trees and other plants just by their common names like an oak, or a lily, or whatever else we have here on Earth. No one is really expecting you to create new plant life.

Creating plants is one of the easiest things to do but it's also one of the most optional. Still, should you do it? Let's take a look at this.

If you're writing science fiction that takes place on a world that's very far removed from Earth, then it's definitely going to have plants that are different from the ones we have here. Even so, people are used to seeing what's essentially an Earthlike planet. While this means that we can get away with not creating plants, maybe it makes more sense if we have at least a handful that are different. The primary reason for this is to make that planet seem like it is not Earth. It's much too easy to just act like it's Earth, but we're calling it a different name, and there is no real difference. By changing the plant life or just adding a few new ones, we can help create the impression of somewhere different.

While this is also true in fantasy, science fiction has the option of having that story have something to do with the Earth, meaning characters from Earth have gone to another world. That world is not going to seem different if we literally don't have something different about it.

Of course, there are other ways to make the world different, such as the number of moons, or the number of planets in the solar system, or even things about that planet itself. One of those would be the plants. This is not to say that we really want to be focusing too much on plants, because let's face it, nobody thinks that plants are really interesting except for people who are into horticulture. We're going to have a story that is about something else, and maybe the plants are just scenery, or maybe one or two of them actually impact the story in some way. We don't need to go crazy this.

You've probably heard the expression that a little bit goes a long way, and this is true of plants and world building. Now if you're thinking that the plants need to be wildly different from those on Earth, they really don't need to be. We're still going to have your basic trees, flowers, and bushes, for example. What we're probably going to want to do is change some of the properties of the ones here on Earth to make them look different, or seem different. This is known as using an analogue, which was discussed in podcast episode number two. By just changing some details, we can save ourselves a lot of the work that might have otherwise happened if we try to create that plant from scratch, so it's really a good idea to take something like a maple tree and then alter a few details.

Before doing analogue, do some basic research on what that plant is like, because you might try to invent one that's based on it and is a little bit different, but the thing that you changed is actually something that does happen on Earth, and maybe you just didn't know that.

For example, let's say that you've never seen anything but a red apple. You invent the yellow apple, not realizing that we actually have those here on Earth. While that color change is still acceptable, you may have it in your head you've done something different from Earth when you actually haven't. Do a little bit of research first.

One of the best reasons to create something new is that we might need something from Earth that has additional properties that it doesn't really have. Maybe we want a plant that can be turned into a narcotic that works differently than anything that's known on Earth. Maybe we want the plant to have healing properties. What if there's a basic ailment that we also suffer from here on Earth, and that in modern times, use something like surgery to fix the problem. But in the world that you're writing, they can't do that. Instead, they use this plant to solve the same problem. Here we have antibiotics. Maybe there they don't have the actual antibiotic, which is created by chemistry, but instead we have a plant that does the same thing. Having a goal like this is a great reason to create a plant.

To help create the feel of something different, plants will help, but they should not be relied upon exclusively. It might help to have three or four plants, a few different animals, a different number of moons in the sky, and use this is part of a bigger picture for differentiation. We should then choose wisely if we're only inventing a few plants. Try to think of ones that can be referenced often, such as a medicine, or maybe there's a kind of wood that is especially good for bows and arrows, for example.

If we also make these plants somewhat rare, then it's more worth it for us to mention it in the context of our story. On the other hand, if the plant is an everyday occurrence, then our characters are not going to notice it and therefore there's less reason for us to mention it. Make sure that your plans count.

In film and television, it's relatively easy to have a number of plants in the background and not make any mention of them. We just need to give them a different appearance and we're good to go. This is also true in gaming. But if the audience is going to be reading our work, then we might want to keep the mention of minor plants to a minimum. Otherwise, we can overwhelm them with many details and make it seem like it's really important when it's not. I have a good example of this.

I have a story called "The Epic of Ronyn." This is available for sale. In this story, there's a moment when the character Ronyn is being pelted with vegetables. When I originally wrote the scene, I named a half-dozen different vegetables that I had created. Some of my beta readers, when they read the scene, said it was just distracting because they had no idea what any of these vegetables were. In reviewing what they said, I decided that it wasn't that important and I just removed that and I replaced them all with the word "vegetables." Obviously, the word "vegetables" is not terribly descriptive. It's not giving you a vivid picture, but I kept the reader from being distracted by something that wasn't that important.

Another option was to explain each one of those vegetables, but it really wasn't the time. If someone's being hit with a bunch of food, this is an action scene, so no one wants to stop and read about them. You have to pay attention to whether it's worth it in any of it seems that you're doing. This is one reason to avoid overdoing it. We might also need to really carefully look for an opportunity to use something and explain it in just a few words, and I have another example of this.

In another story of mine called "The Garden of Taria," two characters have a number of conversations that are important to the plot. These talks take place during a meal. This allowed me to briefly mention some of the food that they were eating. All of the plants and animals were not of Earth. They're all imaginary ones. However, they were all based on Earth. In fact, when I was thinking of what they were eating, I basically decided they were having pork, vegetables, and rice, and I didn't just call them that. I had to use the different versions that I had created.

For example, there's an animal call a tosk. This is the same animal as the one that results in pork (i.e., pig). When the character is cutting into the food, any liquids that were running were clear, as opposed to steak, where it might be red. This allowed me to give a little bit of detail that made the scene a little bit more vivid but also created a sense of somewhere else.

In that same story, there's a scene where the main character comes home to find that another character has made a mess in her home with various foods. I'm going to read a sentence from the story because I want to give you an idea how you can carefully drop words here and there throughout a sentence to get across the idea of a food without just doing an explanation. As I read this sentence, listen for the moment when I emphasize those words.

"She saw a line of *yellow drops* reading from kitchen to couch, discarded *juna peels* discarded here and there along the way, the perpetrator licking the *running juices* from dirty fingers as he popped another *fruit* into his mouth."

The alternative was writing something like, "He ate a yellow citrus fruit called juna." Either one of these is acceptable, but one of them is a little more to the point, and the other one is a little bit more vivid and gets across that they point without having to just explain something.

CLIMATE

When creating a plant, we need to know what climate it is found in. That said, unless our world is made entirely of ice, we can probably assume that every climate exists somewhere on the surface. This means we don't have to figure out what region of the world it is actually found in. We can just decide on its climate, and then when we are working on our world or continent map, and we choose a climate for a region, that will determine whether the plant is there or not.

However, if we already have some idea, this can help us name the plant if we want it to be associated with a given region. This is not to say that it will be found in other places, but sometimes the plants gets a name from one place, even though it's found in others.

CLASSIFICATION

Let's talk about classifying plants. This might not be the most glamorous subject, but by doing this, we can be a little bit more organized and make sure that we don't create 10 of one thing and nothing of another. More importantly, we might think of ideas for one of these categories. That may only happen once we become aware of them, so let's go.

First up are the plants without seeds. This includes algae, liverworts, mosses and ferns, with only mosses being something we're likely to use in our stories, because few people think algae or ferns are very interesting, and hardly anyone knows what a liverwort is, and even if you do, it's not terribly interesting.

As for algae, if we have a sea dwelling creature or species, then we might be able to do something more useful with this. For example, maybe there's a type of algae that is especially deadly, but maybe not to that species, but to humans or other land dwelling species. This underwater species could make use of the poison, such as putting it on their arrows or the rocks they fire from slings. Poison algae doesn't sound very fascinating, but once you turn into a weapon like this, it becomes something more useful. It's also believable and different.

Of course, we could have the algae be something that does impact the species. This could be a positive or negative. Maybe this is poisonous to them, but maybe it's something that heals wounds. We can research algae and decide what circumstances cause this other type of algae to grow.

We can also decide that wizards use this algae in their spells. In science fiction, we can give this algae medical properties that have been harvested.

Algae grows in the water, so that's where we're going to find this. By contrast, moss does not grow in the water so much as near the water. This means it will be found on land. Moss tends to grow on things like rocks and trees, or maybe discarded items.

Moss has a tendency to be green, and in the cases where it's covering a lot of rocks, it can make the landscape look like it's covered in this soft green vegetation, so if we are looking for a reason to have a different color, like purple or red, we can decide that there's a kind of moss that grows that way and therefore it gives this otherworldly appearance to the ground. Let's say we decided we want red, and that this is poisonous.

We can have a famous idea that if the ground has run red, that this means it's going to result in your death. Of course, some people would think of blood, but what they could be referring to is this kind of moss, that if you find yourself walking through it, you're going to die. With some creativity and poetic license, we can do this kind of thing.

The other kind of plants we want to talk about are those with seeds. This includes cycads, conifers, and flowering plants. If you're wondering what a cycad is, so was I the first time I heard the word. Those in tropical and subtropical climates are the ones who are probably more familiar with this. A picture really is worth 1000 words. I would look this up if you can.

To me, it looks kind of like a short palm tree where the fruit is not hanging down from the bottom, but growing on the top. On Earth, these tends to live a long time, such as 1000 years, but on a fictional world we can change this. The fruit that grows on the top, it's easy to imagine a predator wanting to go up there to consume them. And we can give that fruit any property that we desire.

As for conifers, you know the name of a lot of these, such as pines, Cedars, Douglas firs, junipers, redwoods, and spruces. Most of these trees are shaped like cone. The reason for this is so that the snow falls off more easily.

I've saved the best kind for last: the flowering plants. These are the vast majority of plants that you think of when someone says the word "plants." Look out your window and this is what you will see. As a result, this is most of what you're probably going to want to invent. This includes flowers, shrubs, and vines, and trees like the Maple, Elm, Aspen, Birch, and Oak. The deciduous trees are the ones that lose all of their leaves at the same time in the autumn. Now some of you might think that the evergreens never lose their leaves, but they are actually losing them continuously all year such that they always have leaves.

What does all of this classification get us world builders? A better understanding of what to invent: mosses, conifers, and flowering plants. We may have some use for algae and cycads.

USING PLANTS EFFECTIVELY

Let's talk about the ways we can use our plant. You could almost say that there are two types of uses: how we are going to use it and how our characters will. These often overlap. I touched upon this earlier, but one of our uses as an author is to have a plant that has an additional property that an Earth equivalent doesn't have. This could be just wishful thinking on our part, and what I mean is that maybe there's a plant that we wish could do something that it doesn't do. We may have no reason for this other than thinking it's a good idea. And that's fine.

On the other hand, we could be doing it for a story need. This is especially easy in fantasy when we don't have modern medicine, but we wish the characters were able to achieve the same result. We can do that with magic or we can have the gods intervene. Or we can have a plant that achieves the same result. We can do the same thing in science fiction. It's just that the doctors will be extracting whatever properties from a different plant than the ones we have here on Earth.

Medicinal uses are one of the best reasons to invent something. Milk of the poppy from *Game of Thrones* is a good example because this is comes up repeatedly, where it's used to treat characters. They get wounded in fantasy and science fiction far more than in other genres. Making up a plant that had medicinal properties is a great idea because we can have reasons to mention this. And we can also do what George RR Martin did and have a character refuse the treatment because the character is tough and we are characterizing them through this. Or it might not be that the character is so tough, but maybe this drug causes hallucinations and they don't want to experience that because they want their wits about them. On that note, when we are inventing something that has a good property, maybe we also give it a negative side effect like this.

We should also play around with how addictive this substance is. This is a great use for a plant, because we can have characters who are known to be addicted to it. Maybe they are fighting their addiction, or maybe they have lost control to it. Maybe have a character who has become wounded many times and has become addicted to it, or they keep refusing it because they don't want that to happen. We can name friends, family, or others who have had this happen to them. We can even decide that this is something that happens throughout society and that there are people who abstain from it. So now we are starting to create culture that originated from a plant that we created.

Something we can do in fantasy in particular is give some of these plants supernatural properties. This might mean that this plant, or at least part of it, can be used in spellcasting or to make more powerful potions, for example. Such a plant might be considered dangerous. We have a decision to make. Do we want the plant to grow somewhere that it's very hard to reach, and that it's rare, or do we want to have that plant everywhere? Imagine what would happen if this plant was something everyone had easy access to but it was dangerous. Maybe the plant is somewhere heavily guarded as a result.

We might also have one kingdom that has the plant in its territory and another that does not. This could be the reason for war, so now this plant is causing us to create history. Do you still think plants are boring?

Some uses for plants are indeed less interesting, such as decoration. Plants are often used for symbolism. This is true whether the plant is dangerous or associated with peace. We could decide that this plant is known as an aphrodisiac and maybe women wear the plant in their hair at certain times of the year, such as a festival when people are trying to meet their life partner. Once again, we are creating some culture from this.

We should also consider that not all parts of a plant are special. We could decide that it's just the seed, the stems, or the flowering part itself. Decide which part of your invented plant makes it special.

Another basic use for plants is as food. I would suggest making a list of vegetables that your characters might want to eat. Just look in your refrigerator for ideas. Then do a little bit of research on each of them. You might be surprised what you learn and what kind of food is actually made out of something. We don't necessarily eat them raw. We can boil them, fry them, and whatever else. And as I mentioned earlier, we can also have our characters throw them at each other.

How to Get Started

Finally, let's take a quick look at how to get started. I highly recommend starting with an analogue. No matter what you are intending to invent, there is probably something similar here on Earth. You just need to remember the Rule of Three: make at least three important changes. This means not something superficial like just the color. That said, I do believe that changing the color is one of the basic options. It can be hard to think about things to change about a plant. After all, plants are only so complicated.

One way to get started is to create a list of products that might result from plants. This gives us a goal. Maybe we want a poison or an antidote. Maybe we want a medicine to treat a specific problem. There could be weapons that cause certain types of wounds and we only want this type of plant or medication made from it to heal them. We might want a flower that is used during certain kinds of celebrations. Maybe we want an aphrodisiac. Maybe we want a plant that gives someone temporary special powers.

We might also want it to grow in an out-of-the-way location and be very valuable for some reason, such as its supernatural properties, and therefore our characters have to travel to get it despite the great risks of doing so. As far as we know, such a plant might not exist on Earth, and therefore we have to invent one.

Another approach is to create a list of plants that are here on Earth. In this case, we're talking about something specific, such as a rose, nightshade, or a lily. Maybe we are talking trees, like the weeping willow, or pine, or maple. And then of course there are the vegetables, like a tomato, potato, and corn. Do a little bit of research on these and decide if there's any property of them that you would like to remove or add to make them something unique, and how you can use it.

Because let's face it, if you don't have a use for it, there's no reason to create that plant.

HOW AND WHEN TO CREATE ANIMALS

Hello and welcome to *The Art of World Building Podcast*, episode number nine. Today's topic is how to create animals. This includes talking about whether you should do it at all, how to classify them, and what uses we can put them to. This material and more is discussed in Chapter 6 of *Creating Life*, volume 1 in *The Art of World Building* book series.

SHOULD WE CREATE ANIMALS?

The first question we should ask ourselves is whether we need to create animals or if we just want to, and why. If we're doing science fiction and our story takes place almost exclusively on a ship, we may have no reason to invent an animal. After all, it's less likely that they will be walking around. On the other hand, we do have pets here on Earth, and they can stay in our houses, so why not have some pets that can be on a ship?

That said, a pet is not usually considered integral to a plot, but there's no reason we can't change this. How would we do that? Something like a guard dog comes to mind. We can also have pets that have special powers, like the ability to sense certain kinds of radiation or energy. Such an animal might be so useful that it's not a pet but part of the ship, in the sense that maybe the ship is going to travel to certain kinds of places in space where that kind of radiation is expected, and this animal will help them detect it. Most likely, there are other ways of doing that, such as technology, but you get the idea.

We can invent animals that give the person holding them powers. Maybe you can read one person's mind as long as you're holding this animal. Maybe this animal produces something like an egg that if consumed, gives you the power. This could obviously be true in fantasy as well.

And that brings us back to the idea of stories that are not taking place exclusively on a ship, but on a planet that is either Earthlike or not. If the planet is like Earth, then we could just get away with using the same animals that we have here. This means that we could exclusively use existing animals, or mostly use them and invent a handful of our own. Both of these are significantly less work than inventing hundreds of animals. Most of us aren't going to have the time or the desire to do that because most of us are storytellers. Even if we are a gamer, the goal is to create a game that people can play. As always with world building, we want to find a way to create something different while not spending too much time doing that, so it doesn't take away from our real goals.

And on that note, creating something different is one of the main reasons to create animals. Why does this matter? Well, you might want to take your audience out of their comfort zone. If people know how a parrot acts, but you've created a different kind of bird that is similar, they don't know how that bird acts. They therefore cannot predict what that bird might do.

This is true across all of your world building when it comes to life forms, because even standard races like elves and dwarves in fantasy have a typical way that they act. Therefore, people expect certain things. If you create all of your own species and races, no one knows what to expect. For some people, this might be good, and bad for others. This is why it can be good to have a mix of both of these. In other words, use a little bit of what is standard and then add something new of your own.

Behavior

One of the great things about animals is that they act on things, including characters. A major reason to invent our own animal is that if we want to use something from Earth and it doesn't behave a certain way, and we wish that it did, we can use that as an analogue for a new animal of our invention. And that animal has the behaviors that we want.

When we create it, we should change more than one thing about it. I've talked about my Rule of Three when it comes to using analogues. That means create at least three important and distinctive changes from the original. If you are starting with a tiger and you wish that it could be trained like dogs, then create a new version of the tiger, change the way it looks and acts, add a couple other things, and you've got a new animal that is similar but it does what you want and it satisfies the needs you have. By doing an analogue, we've gotten a lot of the work done for us. We just have to do some research. In the case of a tiger, you would want to understand what it can and cannot do. Then make sure that if you are changing things, you know what you're changing. It's like that idea to know a rule before you break it.

One of the things animals do is prey on each other and our species and races. This is another great reason to invent one. We can take an animal that is not normally a man eater and make it be one. We might also decide that only certain species get eaten for some reason. Maybe one of your species has special eyes that are considered a delicacy. Or maybe it's just easier to catch.

Our characters might also acquire certain skills for hunting, attacking, or defending against this predator. We could have a character who grows up around this predator and acquires these skills. Then they go on to become a knight, for example. This is one way to give a character from a rural area fighting prowess that they might not be expected to have. We could have a knight run across this character, get into a fight with him, and be surprised by his skills. We may not have an Earth animal that will cause someone to develop those skills, so this is why we would invent that animal.

One world building question we are often faced with is whether it's worth it. One way to decide is to think about how often you intend to use the setting. If you only use it once, then maybe you don't spend too much time creating things for it. But if you intend to use repeatedly across many works and years, then this becomes more worth it.

If using the setting only once, this is a good opportunity to do something unusual with an animal. After all, if we end up deciding that we don't like what we've done so much, we weren't planning to reuse it again anyway. We can just move on. Otherwise, if using the setting repeatedly, we might be stuck with that animal.

CLASSIFICATION

INVERTEBRATES

Let's talk about classifying the animals we invent. This might not be a very glamorous subject, but it helps us stay organized. This is one of the challenges of world building. Classifying things can also help us decide what to invent.

Something to be aware of is that animals are either invertebrates or vertebrates. This means they are either spineless or not. Otherwise, this has no significance. That said, invertebrates make up 97% of animals. These are the spineless animals. This includes things like worms, sea urchins, snails, jellyfish, arachnids like spiders and scorpions, crustaceans like lobsters and crab, coral, and insects. On Earth, they all tend to be relatively small but we see no shortage of enormous ones in science fiction and fantasy.

Something to consider about the spineless invertebrates is that we are probably not going to use them for domestication, sport, guards, or transportation, unless we do make them truly enormous. This means we might have less use of them. Remember that there are two uses for everything, and what I mean is the author, like yourself, has a use for these creatures, and the characters may or may not have a use for them. If we have no use for what we are inventing, don't invent it.

Our characters may not typically use an animal, but that doesn't mean that they don't interact with it in some way. For example, maybe no one is taking the venom from a scorpion and using it to create poisons, but that doesn't mean that we can't have that scorpion exist and just accidentally sting someone. The character doesn't have a use for it, but we as the creator do.

We may not think insects are interesting because they're so small, but we can create a swarm of them like with locusts. They are known for devouring a huge area of vegetation and causing a problem by doing so. Why is that a problem? Because if you're a farmer and they eat all of your crops, you're kind of in trouble. So is everyone who's counting on your food, like that the local town. In horror films, we often see a swarm that attacks people, but that's not normally what happens, because they don't care and are not carnivores, but there's no reason we can't do that.

VERTEBRATES

I'll spend more time looking at vertebrates, which are the animals you probably thought of when downloading this podcast. They fall into five categories we will look at one by one: amphibians, birds, fish and other aquatic life, mammals, and reptiles.

AMPHIBIANS

Let's talk about amphibians like frogs, toads, and salamanders. There are some basic facts that are similar. They need water to reproduce and they typically need to stay near that water to keep their skin damp. They are also cold-blooded, which means they rely upon their environment to regulate body temperature. This also means that have a slow metabolism, which means they require less food and expend less energy. They also have muscular tongues that can stick out surprisingly far and which are usually coiled up inside their body when not being used.

To avoid being eaten by predators, they can excrete, through glands on their skin, something that either makes them taste bad so that they're spit out, or they're poisonous. Predators will learn a lesson about the latter. The poisonous ones tend to be brightly colored to warn people, so instead of hiding, they're actually announcing their presence. Sometimes that doesn't work, because there can always be a kind of bird, for example, that is immune to the poison and eats them anyway. This happens for real on Earth, so it's definitely an option for your world. If you like this idea, create something like a frog that is this way and decide which species is immune to the poison.

These poisonous amphibians tend to be more active predators because they are less worried about being consumed themselves. By contrast, an amphibian that camouflages itself is more likely to lie in wait and ambush its prey. That prey could be one of your species if the amphibian is truly enormous. Such a large one is probably not too worried about being consumed itself due to its size. Therefore, it might be brightly colored even if not poisonous. However, if it is relying on your species to walk by it without realizing it's present, it will be camouflaged.

Based on this, you could imagine a scene where a group of characters comes across this enormous, possibly red amphibian, and one of them states aloud that they must run away from this. Then someone else responds that it's obviously not a predator due to its color because it would be something that camouflages itself if it was going to eat them, but then he's wrong and they all become a meal.

The Difference between Venom and Poison

Venom must be injected into the body. That's usually from a sting, a bite, or being stabbed. On the other hand, something like a poisonous frog, all you have to do is touch it and the poison could be transferred to you. A very important point here is that poison is used for defense and venom can be used for both defense and offense. If you've decided that an animal is poisonous, that is to protect itself. It's not poisoning its victim. It's poisoning the thing that wanted to make it a victim. On the other hand, something that is venomous is actually a predator who is using that on their prey and for defense. This is one of the reasons why a snake may attack a human even though it has no chance of consuming us.

Make sure you pay attention to this difference and consider its implications when you are inventing a poisonous or venomous animal.

More Classifications

Most amphibians are diurnal, meaning they operate during the day, but some do so at night. Know your rules before you break them. When it comes to their food, virtually all of the amphibians will swallow it whole. If there's any chewing, that's just too subdue the prey.

If you find yourself being hunted by a giant amphibian, there are ways to avoid becoming prey. Most of them hunt by sight and this means that holding still is one way to avoid detection. One problem with this is that most of them can hold still for a very long time, so you would need the ability, too. If you can't take it anymore and decide to run, you might find a very long tongue reaching out, snatching you, pulling you into its mouth, chewing you once or twice to subdue you, and then swallowing you whole. Sounds like fun, doesn't it?

There are more details about amphibians in the *Creating Life* book, but I'm going to save that for the readers.

BIRDS

Let's talk about birds. There are many uses for birds in our fiction. They are often used for symbols, such as the dove for peace, or the hawk for something like war. They can be eaten and so can their eggs. Some birds are also hunted, and we can also create giant birds that can be used for transportation, even though this is likely impossible. We're all used to seeing it, however, and accept it.

There are many are birds on Earth, so it's easy to use one as an analogue and change things such as plumage, behavior (such as how trainable it is), and how rare the bird is. Like amphibians, birds have to swallow food whole because they don't have teeth. Unlike amphibians, they digest things very quickly so that they can fly again. Some birds are also very smart, which could be interesting if you combine that with ferocity and very large size.

Most birds are diurnal but some of them operate at night, twilight, or when the tides are changing as if they feed on animals from the sea. One reason birds form flocks is for safety in numbers. This isn't necessarily an "every bird for himself" kind of thing because, in that scenario, you're thinking that maybe one of your friends gets eaten instead of you, but that's not really the issue. The more birds there are, the more pairs of eyes exist to warn all of them about predators.

You also want to consider whether the bird migrates. The biggest reason is that your characters may be interested in using this bird but it's not all around all year.

FISH

Let's do some classification of fish and other aquatic life. Some of this you may know, but some you won't and other information will act as a refresher.

Fish have fins and gills and are cold-blooded, which means they rely upon their environment to control their body temperature. There's an important distinction to make here and that is that there are animals that have the word "fish" in their name but they are not actually fish. So what is a fish? We're talking about actual fish, eels, lampreys, rays, and sharks, but we're not talking about jellyfish and starfish. Neither of those are fish despite their names. Dolphins and whales are also not fish. Those are mammals.

It may surprise you to know that some fish can actually breathe air just like the rest of us, which means they can go several days without suffocating. Some fish also don't have very good hearing, but some of them are very good at sensing motion. They have very good vision, taste, and smell.

Another characteristic is whether they form a school or a shoal. These are slightly different. A school of fish is one where all of the fish move at the same speed and direction, and change direction at exactly the same time. This makes them appear synchronized. We sometimes see this on nature shows and it usually looks pretty cool. By contrast a shoal is just a group of fish that are in the same area and they are all kind of doing their own thing.

This distinction kind of resonates for me because I recently took up keeping fish in a fish tank. I was told that if I bought six or more of a certain type of fish that they would form a school together. I therefore expected them to be moving in synchronization and they don't do this. They act more like a shoal: they're all in the same general area but doing their own thing. And yes I am disappointed and I want my money back!

How are we going to use this? Well one of the ways is as symbolism. For example, we could have a fish be the reason that a group of starving people didn't perish. Maybe all the food on land was gone due to a drought, but they caught a particular type of fish that saved everybody. There were enough that everyone survived and people came to revere that fish.

But remember that fish are not always good. Sometimes they can sting us, paralyze us, poison us, and sometimes just outright kill us. Sharks come to mind. However, remember that sharks don't typically attack people on purpose. It's usually a case of mistaken identity. However, as a world builder, there's really no reason you can't invent a shark that preys upon your species. Before you do this, you may want to consider a couple things.

For example, normally a shark is feeding on something like a seal, which has a lot of fat and blubber and not much in the way of bones. By contrast, humans have mostly bone. We are really not that appetizing to a shark. You can ignore this, of course, because many filmmakers have sharks purposely eating humans and we have accepted that premise. Know your rules before you break them.

Something to bear in mind is that a shark can kill people by accident, where the shark just does an exploratory bite to see what this thing floating in the water is. But this bite is so severe that it kills a human. Any similar animal that you can create could have the same effect, where they are not actually killing people on purpose. This is one way to be a little more realistic about the danger they pose. We just talked about sharks wanting to eat seals because of the fat content. Having them purposely attack humans to consume us doesn't make as much sense as having them do it accidentally or out of curiosity. This is more believable.

MAMMALS

Let's talk about mammals. They are typically the smartest and largest animals, although we don't have to do that on our invented world. Most of them have four legs, but some of them have adaptations that are so extreme, like dolphins and whales, that we may not realize that they are mammals. Other examples include otters, polar bears, and seals.

Something to consider is that some mammals can exist outside of water, like a polar bear, but others will die. Mammals are warm-blooded and use their own body to regulate their temperature. This can be done in several ways and includes something like blubber, large size, and waterproof fur. Many of us are unfamiliar with this sort of thing and may not realize it on first looking. We might see a polar bear and think it's probably freezing because it's so cold and wet, but it's got the waterproof fur and some fat protecting it. Larger animals also use their weight to stay down on the bottom where their food is, while lighter animals consume food near the surface.

There are also animals like a cat that can spread their body out while they fall so that they are sort of parachuting themselves, slowing their decent. There are also animals that can glide between trees. They are not really flying. They're just able to spread themselves out. We can use some of these traits for our invented animals.

There are some other details discussed in the book but we're not going to cover those here. In the next section, we'll talk about some of what mammals can be used for, such as food, clothing, experiments, pets, transportation, entertainment, and more.

REPTILES

Let's talk about reptiles. This includes turtles, crocodiles, snakes, and lizards. They are cold-blooded, and as you've already heard, this means they rely upon the environment to regulate their body temperature. This also means they have a slow metabolism. They need less food and tend to conserve energy. For that reason, they often have a strategy of lying in wait to ambush prey. The crocodile does this. They can need as much as 90% less food compared to a similar sized mammal.

What if you had a species that was like a human but was based on a reptile? Obviously, they are not going to have the same kind of fast food industry that we have here on Earth because they're not going to be eating all that often. That's a funny example, but this is something that you should consider if you're building a culture that's based on that species, which is based on a reptile. Maybe they are not going to have three meals a day. They might have one big meal or three really small ones, which in turn means that those meals will be over really quick. There might be less formality. These are things to consider and make your work more believable. Bear in mind, that if you've invented an active reptile, then it needs more food. These are the things to research and understand.

Due to this lack of need for food, there are reptiles that can dominate an area if there's not that much food there.

They can eat just once or twice a year whereas a similar sized mammal would need to eat regularly and there isn't enough food there to sustain one. You could have characters traveling through a desolate area with no livestock and reach the conclusion that there probably aren't any predators when there really are, and they're reptiles. If you're thinking that most reptiles are carnivores, you are correct, but herbivores do exist, so this is an option.

Reptiles tend to have smaller brains. As a result, they are less intelligent. Most of them are diurnal, meaning they are active during the day, but some are active at night. By knowing this, we once again have another option to use.

Smaller reptiles will usually rely upon camouflage to avoid being eaten. Some of them will make a noise like the rattlesnake, and then there's the cobra, which will make itself look bigger by fanning out part of its body. Something that's really interesting, especially if you have a humanoid species that's based on a reptile, is that some reptiles can detach their tail so that they can escape. Sometimes the tail will be brightly colored to attract the predator to that part of the body. Why? Because they're hoping that if they are attacked, it's at the tail, which they can detach while they run away. Meanwhile, the predator is distracted by the still wiggling tail in its mouth.

These tails can also regrow, but sometimes they're a little bit discolored and don't grow back to the same length.

How to Use Animals

Let's start wrapping up talking about how can we use the animals we've invented. After all, if neither us or our characters have a use for them, what's the point?

Domestic work is one use for them. This includes pulling wagons. This isn't very glamorous but this can be a good place to start with inventing animals because it's something that's not more prominent most of the time and we can get some experience inventing a less important animal. If you've never created an animal before, maybe this is where you start.

You might be thinking that this is not worth it, but you can create the impression of somewhere different by citing different animals pulling that wagon train. In science fiction, such animals may have been replaced by machines. This certainly suggests that we have less use of them. However, they still could be a symbol of former times, such as an ox being seen as a stable animal. A company might use this as a symbol. A character may use this as a nickname. This is still true in science fiction and fantasy.

Another use for animals is as entertainment or sport. This could be because we are hunting them, or racing them against each other, whether we are riding them or not. Horses come to mind. They can be used for riding them, racing them, or as pack animals pulling a wagon. We can have multiple uses for one animal. The names of such animals can also be used for ships or sporting things. The Broncos and Colts from the National Football League come to mind. Bronco is also the name of a vehicle, while Colt is the name of a gun.

Of course, there is food. We might decide that some of our animals are not very good to eat, but for the most part, many of them will be, and they will taste different from each other. We can just invent the quality of the meats, such as whether it is tender or tough. We can also decide that people prepare it certain ways. If you're not sure how to cook tough meat, then you can just research this.

Many animals used as food are kept in pastures, so this is something we might mention while our characters are approaching a town or farm, for example. This isn't a very exciting, but the little detail can add some realism. If you were approaching a farm on Earth, you would probably see cows and horses in the field. This, in turn, might tell you something about the farm that you are approaching. We can do the same thing. Not all animals can be kept in a pasture because of their aggressive nature.

Hunting scenes are a classic staple of fantasy and science fiction. We might want to invent animals that must be hunted. The capturing and killing of such an animal can be considered a heroic or great thing for our character to do. It's something that shows his strength or virility.

Sometimes the animals in pastures are docile unless they are approached, in which case they may act differently and become aggressive. If there's a nearby predator who feeds on the animal, the animal could sense or smell it and it might start howling. This can be an indication to the characters that there is a dangerous predator nearby, one that might prey upon them, too. In other words, this is an early warning device. This could be one reason people keep certain animals around their home.

As an example of this, I've always had cats, and sometimes I will hear a noise in the house. My cat will hear it, too, and perk up. The cat will casually look over and go back to what it's doing, which tells me there's nothing for me to worry about. But there are times when the cat gets freaked out, and that's when I go to investigate. Dogs are famous for barking at things, but sometimes they do it when there's no threat at all.

There are other uses for animals that I'm not going to go into detail here, but they are discussed in the book. This includes as guards, materials, pets, and transportation.

WHERE TO START

I want to wrap up on where to start with inventing animals. Analogues are a great way to get started and I highly recommend this for animals. Most of us have neither the time nor the interest in becoming an expert in certain kinds of animals. We don't want to invent something from scratch, so it's a lot easier to take something that's similar to what we want and modify it. This avoids the problem of inventing something that doesn't make any sense.

Remember the Rule of Three when inventing an analogue: make at least three significant changes. If you don't do this, people are going to recognize that it's really an Earth animal with minimal changes. This can actually backfire on us instead of transporting the audience to another world with something that's different, it just makes us look like we're doing a poor job of this. We don't really care. They recognize the source for what it is.

Make sure you do your research before using an analogue because many things on Earth are different from what we think. This is because we only have a casual understanding of what they're like. This research doesn't need to be time-consuming. Much of it can be off of Wikipedia, although you should try to verify that what you're reading is correct, but if you are going to use an analogue, you almost don't have to worry about it too much because you're going to alter it anyway.

Another way to get started is to create a list of animals that you would like in your world. For example, we could list some mammals like boar, deer, bear, cow, or goat. For sea life, we might want something like a shark, whale, rays, regular fish, flying fish, and dolphins. For lizards, we might want a snake or several, and crocodiles. For birds, we could use a vulture, pigeon and a falcon.

We have some variety in that list I just mentioned. For the birds, a vulture is good for flying above a battle scene looking for something to eat. Our characters can approach the site of a battle that ended in the last day, and these birds are circling overhead, and that's the first indication from a distance that there was something going on. By contrast, a pigeon is mostly just a pest to most of us. It might be something we encounter at the seashore. A hawk or a falcon is something we might use for hunting. Here we have three different uses for birds. The characterization of them is very different.

My point here is to invent something with a variety. Don't create a hawk and a falcon, for example. Those are very similar. Keep this in mind when making your lists.

Another approach is to create a products list. These will result from these animals. Our characters can use them and we can reference them in scenes. For example, goats are used to make cheese and cows can make milk. Just research some of the basic animals that you are aware of to learn what kind of products result from them.

Hopefully with all of this information, you have a good idea for how to get started with inventing animals.

HOW TO
CREATE UNDEAD

Hello and welcome to *The Art of World Building Podcast*, episode number ten, part one. Today's topic is how to create undead. This includes talking about whether you should do it at all, how to classify them, and how the origins affect them. This material and more is discussed in Chapter 7 of *Creating Life*, volume 1 in *The Art of World Building* book series.

SHOULD WE CREATE UNDEAD?

As is often the case with a world building subject, the first thing we should consider is whether we should create something. And in this case, that's undead.

Most ideas we have about undead are public domain, so we can use them. No one else owns it. This is true of vampires, zombies, ghosts, skeletons, and more. While all of those are public domain, there might be an idea that you might want to use and you're not sure, in which case, you should just Google it. If it is public domain, then you can use it. But if it's not, you're going to have to make some alterations if you want to do something similar.

Remember my Rule of Three - make at least three important changes to an analogue so no one realizes what it is. This will reduce your risk of being accused of plagiarism. Remember that these three or more changes should be significant and not something as trivial as a color. That said, we can change basic appearance and its origins, not to mention the most important thing, which is its behavior. One thing about these standard ideas is that they are widely accepted and no one is going to roll their eyes that you are yet another person using them. There is arguably less expectation for new undead types from the public.

On the other hand, in science fiction, we tend to expect new species and races. Why do we have that expectation? Well, if the story is not connected to Earth in any way, then we're only going to have humans and probably other species. Even if the story is connected to Earth, but people are traveling very far from home, as is often the case with *Star Trek*, then we're going to expect them to encounter new life forms. By contrast, the expectation for standard undead seems to be almost universal. The primary reason for this might be simply that some people don't invent undead. On the other hand, a show like *Star Trek* so often has a new species to the point where it's almost like a "species of the week" kind of thing. Almost like *The X-Files* had the "monster of the week" sort of thing going on that we just expect it. In the end, I think that we are pleasantly surprised when someone shows us a new type of undead.

Maybe more of us should do that, and learning how to do it well is the goal of this podcast episode and the following one that will continue the subject. Since there is no backlash to using existing undead, you should do this unless you have a good reason not to. Inventing anything takes time and effort that is maybe better spent on story craft, for example. But the most important decision point is whether you have an idea or not. Because if you don't have one, then what's the point?

You should think about how you're going to use this undead. If you're thinking of a ghost that's going to do typical ghost behavior, then just use a standard ghost. You could call it something else and this is fine but when doing so, you may want to have given it a property that is unexpected. This could be its appearance or behavior.

There is a direct correlation between how many changes we make and whether we give it a new name. The more changes we make, the more we justify a new name. On the other hand, if we make almost no changes and we give it a new name, that may actually be off-putting to some people. We might get their hopes up that this is a new interesting thing and then it's just something that they've already seen before. In other words, it can cause a backlash.

If using a known name for something like a vampire, we should consider whether or not we have made a fundamental change and therefore should not use that name. In the case of a vampire, if it doesn't drink blood, this is too basic a change. You probably shouldn't call it a vampire. You could still do it, but it's ill-advised. Your audience may not like it. There's a good way and a bad way to defy expectations, and this is probably the bad way.

Should you create undead? Probably not. But if you're still curious, the rest of this episode and the next will probably give you some ideas on how to go about doing so.

OUR UNDEAD'S MIND

The next thing I want to talk about is the mind. After all, the mind is going to control much about this undead and how it acts. And this mind could be present or absent to one degree or another depending on what we believe about whether the mind goes with the soul (if one exists) when someone dies or whether that comes back with them if they are reanimated. If you believe in the soul and the afterlife, I think most of us assume that the mind basically goes with the soul. Otherwise, concepts like having Heaven and Hell have no meaning. After all, if your mind is absent then you can't exactly enjoy the pleasures of Heaven and being reunited with lost loved ones. And if you're in Hell, then you're not going to be able to appreciate the torture. Now some torture is physical and in theory you would be able to experience that, but of course the horror of that is going to be significantly more pronounced if you are mentally capable of really perceiving it. Some torture is more psychological and emotional and both of those aren't going to work as well if you've got no mind.

So let's say for the sake of argument that the mind goes with the soul upon death. This exercise brings up some interesting scenarios, and we can use this to our advantage when inventing a new type of undead. Based on this idea, we can probably assume that a ghost has its mind. After all, a ghost is considered to be a spirit or a soul. Now just because a mind is present does not mean that there is nothing wrong with that mind. Any number of things could have traumatized it.

Depending on the manner of one's death, that certainly could have done it. This is especially true if you were murdered, for example. The opposite extreme would be dying peacefully in your sleep. We can imagine all sorts of incidents in between these two extremes that would cause someone's mind to be a little bit impaired. Or depending on our purposes, very impaired.

Once dead, that could also cause trauma depending on where one went. For example, if you went to Hell and you were being tortured, before you returned to being just a soul wandering the Earth, that is obviously going to be something upsetting to you.

On the other hand, if you went on to an afterlife that was more pleasant like Heaven, then in theory, that's going to be something that's comforting to you. Or at least, that's how we typically see Heaven is a place where everyone is at peace. But it could certainly still be upsetting to discover that you're dead. And while it's great that you're reunited with your loved ones, for example, there's still the reality that all of you are dead. If you're reunited with someone you haven't seen in fifty years, that could be kind of upsetting in some way. Maybe their personality isn't even what you thought it was or what you remember. Or maybe someone you expected to be here isn't there, because they're in Hell instead, so that could certainly upset you.

We like to believe that Heaven is a place where nothing is going to upset us, but we have options when it comes to this. The basic idea here is that the time one is not alive or undead could also be a period of in between time. That might be upsetting and alter the mind in some way. If you are in this in between place for let's say hundreds of years, and before you become a spirit that's wandering somewhere, then that would presumably cause you to have extensive experience being in that state. And then you were suddenly thrust into a new state of being a wandering spirit. The simple fact of a change having taken place after such a long time and already adjusting to another major change could also cause a lot of distress. And of course we have the option of an instantaneous change from death to being a ghost. We don't necessarily have to have a long time in between, but it's an option.

Of course, some undead have a body, and possibly a mind as well, and it could face the same problems. On the other hand, what if the body does not have a soul in it? That would suggest it doesn't have a mind either. Maybe it's only as intelligent as an animal. Either way, we can use this to rationalize what our undead is capable of. There's one specific way that a ghost can be mentally impaired and that is by denying that it is dead. Logically, this might seem difficult to do if you're a spirit, but that might be because we are assuming that the spirit is, for example, floating in the air or it's passing through solid objects, or it just looks like a white sheet or something, not a white sheet, but you know how a ghost is often depicted as being white. If it looked down on itself or its outstretched arm, it wouldn't see the normal arm that we had when we were alive. It would see this white arm. Well, that's just a popular depiction of ghosts, which is not real to most of us. I'm leery of saying that, because some of you are going to say, "Yes, they are!" But for most of us, this is just an imaginary thing that we have invented to tell stories.

And we have invented this typical appearance as well, but it doesn't have to be that way. There are many old ghost stories where the ghost appears like a living person. They are still dressed. They still have a normal skin tone, and for all practical purposes, from at least a distance, you cannot tell that you're looking at a ghost instead of a living person. This idea is equally common in ghost stories, and it's something that we can use. One justification for a ghost looking this way is that if it doesn't realize that it's dead, then it's retaining its self-image from life. That means that its appearance is a projection from its own mind.

These ghosts often will pass right through objects, but that's not because they realize it's doing so. The idea is often that it doesn't realize that something is different from when it was there in life. For example, if the ghost is haunting a place where it lived and renovations had been made, there might be a wall where there used to be a hallway. And this ghost goes right through the wall, because it doesn't recognize that the wall is there. This is a justification for having a ghost do ghostly things without it being aware that it is dead.

Another common idea for ghosts is that they are going about a behavior that they carried out in life, as if they are still alive. The big problem with inventing a ghost that does this is that we are not inventing a ghost that does this. It's a common idea.

Such a ghost may not be tormented by the fact that it is dead, because of course it is in denial that it's dead. Or maybe it's going about these repeated behaviors to prove to itself that it's still alive. Regardless, what this demonstrates is that something is not quite right about this ghost's mind. It is mentally impaired. A ghost may be well aware it is dead and behave in a very different fashion while also having a different projection of its self-image. Maybe we are implying something about the ghost's mind when we show what it looks like. A particularly cunning ghost might even use that as a way of fooling people. If I was a tormented ghost who wanted to wreak havoc on the living, I might initially present myself in a peaceful manner. And with my body image reflecting that I think I'm still alive before surprising somebody. If you decide to invent a new type of undead, give some serious thought to its mental capability.

CLASSIFYING UNDEAD

Let's talk about classifying undead.

The first choice we should make is whether it has a body or not. If it does have a body, the word "undead" is most often used, and this implies that it has a body that is animated once again. If it has no body, it is usually called a spirit or ghost. For the rest of this episode and the next, we're going to use the word spirit to mean it has no body. We'll use the word corporeal to mean it has a body, whether it has a soul or not. And we'll use the word undead to generically refer to both of these.

Spiritual undead are theoretically more limited, because they don't have a body, and therefore can't touch anything. However, we've all heard of stories where they supposedly can, under usually extreme circumstances, such as being very upset. This gives us the option to have the spirit normally unable to touch anything, but under certain circumstances it can. We might find it useful to give a limitation this way but then have an option to overcome it at times.

We could decide that the ability to physically affect the world will weaken a spiritual undead. They could get more vulnerable. We can decide that it can pass through objects, which is an advantage, but that it cannot move them, which is a disadvantage. And by doing this, we can basically balance out this spirit, so that it can't do *everything*.

Making decisions this way is one way we can invent a new kind of spirit. Something else we might consider is where the spirit's body is. Maybe the spirit wants to reanimate it or repossess that body. Maybe the body has something about it that is unique, such as an ability. Maybe when the spirit last saw its own body, it had something like a magic item or a weapon of technological origin, and this is something that it desires. Of course, this is only an option if the spirit recognizes that it is dead.

As for corporeal undead, they come in two varieties - those with a soul and those without. If the mind goes with the soul and the soul is absent, that could explain the mental capabilities of our undead. Maybe this is why zombies act the way they do. All of this is make believe, but thinking about it this way can give you ideas.

Our corporeal undead may have senses that are altered, either for the better or worse. It seems logical that senses would be worse. After all, things like taste, smell, and sight are going to be affected by the body having decayed. However, we generally accept that if undead exists, there is some supernatural agent at work here, and that same agent could have given super senses to the undead.

Maybe it can smell human flesh farther away than it would have in life whether that flesh is alive or decaying. This could allow it track others of its kind or the living to attack. Perhaps it sees better now but only in moonlight. Maybe they can hear farther away than they could before, and now they can eavesdrop on conversations, learning things they never would have known before.

These new abilities could give them a feeling of power and also alter their mental state. Maybe they feel cocky now. In theory, being dead means that we have a loss of our bodily functions. However, the case of *Dracula* and other vampires by extension shows that we are willing to accept an undead that looks just like it's alive and can do everything that we can do. In some recent stories, we've even seen vampires giving birth.

The point here is that we can decide for ourselves whether an undead is a vision of health, a rotting corpse, or a skeleton. It's really up to us. We can get away with extremes, and the best example of this is the living skeleton. It doesn't have any muscles to control its body, not to mention the brain, but yet it can do all sorts of things. This always implies something supernatural, otherwise it doesn't make any sense.

For corporeal undead that have more of a body but one that is still decayed, that decay would seem to explain the hampered movement. On the other hand, we've all seen zombie movies where the zombies are running around just like they are perfectly healthy.

Something to consider when it comes to corporeal undead is how long it has been dead. There's a tendency to assume that the longer something that is dead the more it has decayed, but that doesn't really have anything to do with it. The exposure to air and the amount of water in the soil around it is partly responsible for how fast something decays. We don't want to get too technical about it, but something could be dead for a thousand years and look relatively well-preserved. On the other hand, something could be dead and exposed to the elements for only a few years and be a bare skeleton.

Try not to fall into this trap of thinking that the age of corporeal undead has something to do with its appearance. I think this is actually good news for us world builders, because it gives us a little more freedom to just decide something is the way it is and that's kind of all there is to it. No one is expecting us to explain the level of aridity in the soil, for example.

While we don't have to justify it, bear in mind that some people will probably try to call us out anyway and say, "Well, that doesn't make any sense." And we will know better, but we do run the risk of that kind of reaction from people who think that they know everything.

Let's talk about non-sentient undead. What do I mean by that? Plants and animals. If you think that an undead plant doesn't seem very terrifying, I kind of agree with you on that one. On the other hand, most of us have seen the

Lord of the Rings and the Ents, which are giant trees that can walk and talk and do other things. So there's no reason one of them can't be turned into undead. If it was once alive, it can be dead, and if it can be dead, it can be undead.

Most of us think that plants don't have a soul, which means that spiritual undead are not an option. Since plants can't change their location, it's pretty easy to get away from one or stay away from one, unless we change this. Earlier, we talked about supernatural elements being present in all undead, so wouldn't it be interesting if a plant had not been sentient but now that it is undead, it is sentient. That opens up some options you can explore.

Finally, let's talk about undead animals. Just like the supernatural can give plants the ability to be sentient, maybe we can give animals the ability to speak, for example. That adds a new level of horror to encountering one of them. We've often seen them be given great strength or speed, and these are clichés but they are done to make them more formidable. Sometimes, they appear to have an increased ability to work in conjunction with each other. Something that can be fun about undead animals is that maybe now that they are reanimated they want to feed on something they didn't use to feed on, such as our new species and races. It may not have a sinister purpose behind doing so.

Another classic idea is of the undead animal that bites a living person, who then becomes undead. The only problem with this idea and some of the others we've been discussing is that none of these are new. However, it's still a good idea to keep these in mind, and one of the reasons for that is that we can take all of these different elements and combine them into something new. Sometimes being original means piecing things together in a novel way, not necessarily inventing things that have not been done at all. This might be our best bet with inventing undead.

THEIR ORIGINS

One thing I'm not going to discuss in this particular epi-sode, but which is discussed in the book, is how many of this particular undead type exists and the effect this has on them. Another subject we will not cover is whether there are prerequisites for this type of undead or not, and how someone might prevent themselves from becoming one.

The final subject we want to talk about today is the ori-gins of our undead. Knowing where the undead originated is often a basic part of their identity, and this is one of the ways we can make them original. After all, if we've created a world or more than one world where there are unique phenomenon or technologies, then this gives us an oppor-tunity to create a specific type of undead. The more unique the world and the lifeforms that live there, the more unique the types of undead we might have.

A good story behind our undead type also makes it more interesting. Our two basic options are accidental un-dead and those that are created on purpose. Whether it's nature, supernatural, or technological forces, it's pretty easy to create undead by accident, and yet it's never hap-pened here on Earth. Imagine that.

In theory, most undead will be accidental, because even if someone actually wants undead to exist, they prob-ably don't also have the skills to make that happen. On the other hand, if they somehow caught and trapped an un-dead type and that undead has the ability to do something like bite someone and turn them into an undead type, then someone could still do this.

However, that doesn't explain the original origins of that undead type. And on that note, we don't necessarily have to reveal where it came from. It's entirely possible that nobody knows. No explanation is certainly the easiest but is not necessarily the most satisfying, so if you happen to think of a good explanation, that's better. Unless of course, you would like a mystery. However, with every good mystery, we usually want to find out the answers sooner or later, and the reveal should be good. Otherwise, we've disappointed everyone.

So it might be best to have figured this out first, especially because knowing the origins can really help us invent something interesting. Just like with monsters, an undead that has resulted from an accident might want revenge on the person or people who created that accident in the first place. This gives it a goal, and we'll talk a lot more about goals in the next episode.

One thing about an accident is that if it's something like an explosion, this could affect a lot of people in the same area. This is the easy way to justify many of them existing. In time, these undead may spread out and cover the entire world, especially if they can replicate themselves. Absent a large scale explosion to create many of them at the same time, each one of these undead type might be rare, and if something is rare, especially if there's only one of them, it might be particularly hard for anyone to figure out how to deal with it. Why? Because maybe they've never encountered it before. There might be no record of what to do or how to kill it.

We could also decide that specific types of phenomenon are known to cause specific types of undead. We talked a little about this in a previous episode about creating monsters, but the same idea holds true. It's possible that the location of such phenomenon is subsequently guarded so that no one can have this happen anymore. The phenomenon might also be destroyed in some way so that it can't happen again.

Finally, let's talk about the undead by design. When someone wants to create one on purpose and has the ability, one question we should ask is whether the perpetrator is able to control the result. Such an undead could be sent to do anything we can think of. If our perpetrator cannot control the undead, then he might end up the first victim of it. This means that there won't be any more of that type of undead unless it has the ability to replicate itself.

Then again, maybe this person left a journal for how they were doing it, and this is later discovered by others. Such a person might be trying to do something else and accidentally created the undead. What if our perpetrator was unhappy with what he had done and tried to destroy it? Did he chase it away, or did it retaliate and kill him or wound him? What if it turned him into the first duplicate? What about how the undead feels about its new status? Does it like being a servant? Probably not. Does it like being undead? Probably not. It may chafe at its new role and want revenge or to be freed from it, and this is another goal that we'll talk about in the next episode.

HOW TO
CREATE UNDEAD

Hello and welcome to *The Art of World Building Podcast*, episode number ten, part two. Today's topic concludes our discussion about how to create undead. This includes talking about their goals, traits, how to kill them, and what uses we can put them to. This material and more is discussed in chapter 7 of *Creating Life*, volume 1 in *The Art of World Building* book series.

WHAT DO YOUR UNDEAD WANT?

Even the undead want something. Today, we're going to talk a little bit about what they might want and why. Just because someone is dead doesn't mean that all their desires have left them. But, this will depend on the desire. It's probable that they don't have desire for food, for example. So, someone who was a glutton in life is not going to have that preoccupation in death, most likely. But, you never know. They might have a ravenous appetite for something else. In the case of vampires, that would be blood.

This brings up the question of whether an undead type needs some sort of sustenance from the living, or even just from the world that it inhabits, in order to remain in its current state. We'll talk about that a little bit more later when discussing traits, because the ability to consume something is one of those traits. That said, a goal for any undead would be to continue its existence. Now, by that, I don't mean that it wants to remain undead because that could be very unpleasant. But, if it converts into a living person or goes back to being just fully dead, that is still some sort of existence. So, it might have a desire to go from being undead to alive, or being undead to dead, or just remaining undead. Any of these could be a goal.

Why might death be a preference? Well, if being undead is just extremely unpleasant, that's an obvious choice, but there's also the reality that this person who is now undead could've come from a pleasant afterlife like heaven. And, as a result, this is horrible by contrast. It's possible that some undead are that way by choice, but many of them will not be. So, someone who was in heaven probably doesn't want to go from that to being undead because it's probably not a positive change for them.

That does bring up an interesting idea. What if you could willfully go back and forth between being in heaven and being undead? How and why someone might want to do that, I'll leave up to you, but it's an idea that I'm going to throw out there. It's possible that someone might enjoy being an undead because they are very powerful. And the example that comes to mind are vampires. A common idea that we often see is that someone doesn't want to die and become a vampire, but, once they become one, they are suddenly infused with all this power and super senses, and they kind of enjoy it.

We typically see that transformation from dead to vampire as being nearly instantaneous, so it's not like the person spent 20 years or even 1 year inside a place like heaven before becoming a vampire. But, it's a possibility we could certainly do. There's no rule saying that someone who is dead for a long time cannot be resurrected as a vampire. It doesn't have to be a vampire, of course. It could be an undead type of our own invention, which is the point of this podcast episode. So, we can create something where this has happened, where someone who's dead becomes a new type of undead that we have created. And, as that type of undead, they are very powerful, and they actually enjoy being undead.

I do have to say, though, that my personal preference is not to make the undead state be something that's really cool. You know, we see this a lot in a lot of the modern vampire TV shows, for example. And it takes the whole idea of being dead or undead and turns it into some great holiday or something. And I think it kind of fundamentally goes against the idea of horror in undead. So, it's something to consider.

If you decide to go this route and make the undead state be somehow enjoyable, you should still probably try to find a way to make it also a torment for that character. There certainly might be individuals who enjoy this, but there are going to be others who find it horrifying. It's going to really depend on the character of that person before this happened, and even their character after it happened because something like death and then reanimation as undead could certainly change one's personality, especially if you gained super powers when it happened.

I just want to caution against making undead some idealized state. There may be people in that undead state who are romanticizing how great it is and sort of ignoring the reality of it, in some cases, and they may be trying to trick the living into thinking it's great so that someone voluntarily becomes that kind of undead. You know, it's one of the things that we think about with undead, especially with vampires, is the way they seduce people. And this is another version of that.

What I'm getting at is that some undead characters might think it's great and honestly believe that, and others will just be trying to trick the living into becoming one of them. Because, of course, misery loves company.

One of the things that we see in the world of vampirism that we can leverage for our own undead type is the idea that if a vampire creates another vampire subservient to it, that vampire actually becomes physically or spiritually stronger. This is a good motivation for an undead to lie to the living. If converting you into that kind of undead makes me more powerful and makes my misery less miserable, then sure, I'm going to lie to you.

So, there's a difference between the idea of it being romanticized and the reality of it being actually horrible, and I think that this is a viable way to go if you would like to have characters who are acting like it's great. But, having it be actually great, that might not be the smartest or most believable idea. Some listeners might think that the idea of being believable is out the window because we're talking about something as make-believe as undead, but making something believable actually makes our inventions more credible and understandable for the audience.

Make it believable and you may it better.

MORE GOALS

An undead type may want to go back to being dead so that it can get some rest or go back to a pleasant afterlife. On the other hand, if that afterlife was one where it was being tortured, then probably it doesn't want to go back. This is one reason why you may want to consider how long someone who is living must be dead before they become this type of undead, and don't be afraid to decide that it can typically be one way, but then, sometimes, it's another way. For example, with vampires, they usually go from living to dead for just maybe a minute before they become undead, and maybe we decide that that's what typically happens. But then, there's a case where someone's dead for a year and then they somehow come back.

I'm using vampires as an example, but you can do this with any undead type of your invention. But, what about regaining life? Is this something that an undead might want? Sure. Why not? If you're walking around this world as undead, surrounded by the living, you probably want to get back to that state. That won't be true of everyone, but this kind of goes back to what I was talking about earlier where if being undead is unpleasant, then you probably will want to stop being in that state. And there are plenty of people who will say that life is unpleasant, but we should probably decide that undead is significantly worse. And, therefore, however much you might want to complain about how life was for you, you have a second chance here and it's going to be better than being undead.

Your undead may say they prefer being undead, but they might just be thinking that because they had a horrible life. If given the chance for a new life where it could turn out better, and they have all the knowledge that they have now – you know, we often ask that question, "Would you do it over again?" – they may decide to choose life.

Let's say, for the sake of argument, that an undead type does want life. Well, how are they going to go about this and what challenges do they face? If you are a spiritual undead, the first problem you need to solve is where are you going to get another body? In most cases, your old one is dead and probably not much use. Now, it's possible that it's being kept in some sort of stasis chamber, because we've got that option in science fiction in particular, but, in most cases, the body, the original, it's no good.

This will certainly be impacted by how you died. If your head was cut off, well, reanimating that body's not going to do you much good because you're just going to die immediately again anyway. Even if you died peacefully of old age, well, that body is done. So, you can't use it again. There are very few scenarios where you could reuse that body. Any sort of injury or disease that ruined it and caused you to die is still, essentially, in effect, even if you reanimate it minutes later.

And the timeframe brings up an important issue because the body starts decaying and becoming useless quickly. The odds are that your old body is not an option. However, that said, in SF and fantasy, we have an option, such as technology or magic, that could restore that body. The issue is that you're going to want to get that body restored before you reanimate it. So, how are you going to convince someone who has a life to do this for you? Or does your spiritual undead have the ability to manipulate physical objects such as a device that would do this?

Now we're starting to get into something plausible. If it doesn't have the ability to take care of this itself, then it's probably going to have to appear as an apparition that appears alive, possibly, or as an obviously, spiritual undead to some person who has the ability to make this happen. Is that person going to cooperate? Well, it's going to depend on who they are. If it's a family member and they miss you, then maybe. If it's your enemy, then no. Unless, of course, you have some ability to threaten that person.

Being threatening fits more into the idea of what undead are like because these are supposed to be frightening, right? That brings up an interesting scenario, though. What if, as a spirit, you are able to threaten this person into restoring you to life, but then you re-inhabit your body and, as soon as you do that, you lose the ability to threaten that person, and then they kill you? It's easy to imagine a story where someone doesn't realize that could happen, but the person they've been threatening does, and that's the outcome. Or is our spirit thinking that far ahead? If so, then it's a little bit more wily.

Now, one thing to be aware of is, if the body could be restored this way, it begs the question of why wasn't this done when the person was alive? And the easy answer for that is that something happened too quickly, and the person died. Medical, magical or technological intervention was unable to do this in time. We have another possible issue there, and that is that if someone's body is burned to ashes, is the technology good enough to restore them from that state, or does the body have to be in a state that's a little bit closer to normal? You may want to decide on some sort of limitation like this to, again, make it more believable and like your characters don't have just incredible options at their disposal.

A story where characters find it too easy to get by or get around a situation is one that just lacks conflict. Generally, you don't want to make things too easy for them. Creating a restriction might seem like it's no fun, but what happens is that this gives your character something that they have to work around, and this causes plot, storyline and actions. Generally, this is one way that you can move your story forward, by creating a limitation.

What if restoring the body is not an option? What else can they do? How about possess somebody? Even if the individual's body is available, it could, instead, try to take someone else's. One question is whether the target body needs to have a soul in it for this to happen. This is normally what we assume, but there's no reason it has to be the case. There could be reasons that a spirit is missing. For example, someone could be having an out-of-body experience, which we often think of as the soul being gone. During that time, what if somebody took over your body? Now you're the one who doesn't have a body to go back to.

This might seem farfetched, and, of course, the whole thing is, but I have a species that has the ability to willfully separate its soul from its body. If I were living on that world and I was a spiritual undead, I would probably hang out with members of that species while I'm undead and then try to take over one of them once one of them leaves their body. In the cases where there is another soul in that body, now we've got a situation where there are two of them. A standard idea here is which one of those spirits is stronger than the other one, and which one of them can take over.

Something we should consider is what happens to the one who gets suppressed? Does the invading spirit get expelled or does it remain trapped in that body, but it's now being dominated by the person it tried to take over? It might find that, rather than improving its situation, it has now made it significantly worse. However, what storytellers have typically done is decide that the invading spirit is the stronger one for whatever reason. After all, that's one of the reasons why it has managed to cling to this undead state rather than going to an afterlife. This implies it has a certain amount of strength and, therefore, it's stronger than the average person, since what usually happens is someone goes to the afterlife. Since it didn't do that, it's therefore, stronger. And, therefore, once it invades someone else's body, it is strong enough to suppress the soul that's already in there.

The only real problem with this idea is that this is not something new. So, we wouldn't be inventing this if we decide to do this. However, as I mentioned in the previous episode, combining ideas into something new is an option.

What happens if someone is successful at acquiring a new body, whether it's theirs or not? Now what? If it's their old body and they decide to reacquaint themselves with their former acquaintances, then how are people going to react to their appearance, especially if they are known to be dead and they have been buried? Your answer to this may depend on how common it is for someone to reanimate their body this way. If it's never been done, or hardly ever, then people will probably have a strong negative reaction. If it's common, then they might think, "Oh, why did it take you so long to reanimate your body? We've been expecting you."

What if they try to go and get back all their worldly possessions? Have they all been sold? Has their house been given to somebody? They're not going to be able to reacquire all this stuff. Once again, this will depend upon how long they were dead before becoming undead, and then regaining life. If it is common for people to come back like this, then maybe there are laws that you can't give away someone's stuff for about a year. Do they get back any of their rights now that they have returned? In the United States, at least, people are declared legally dead. But, if you reappear, then what is your option here? What if they've got a new body and they try to reinsert themselves into their old life that way? No one's going to recognize them. Are they even going to try to pretend that they are their old self in a new body, or are they just going to pretend that they are this new person whose body they're in now?

The attempt at doing so might have them showing undue familiarity with someone they just met. That other person will think that they're strangers, but this new undead person who is now alive again will be very familiar with them. There are other, similar questions that we can explore about this, and more of them are in the *Creating Life* book. Have a look if you are looking for more options.

What about undead that have a body? Since the body is moving around, they may have the ability to restore their own body. A device that does this makes this especially easy for them. On the other hand, they still might need someone else to do it for them, and they are still going to need the ability to threaten that person if they don't want to cooperate. Once their own body is restored, they have all the same problems that we already just discussed.

In the last episode, we talked about the option of a corporeal undead that has no soul in the body. Whether this person can return to life is an academic debate that I will leave for you. However, it does beg the question that we went over in the last episode, and this is if the mind goes with the spirit and the spirit is not in this body, is this body even going to be smart enough to think of this plan? And, if it does, it if works, how is this body going to get its soul back if its soul is somewhere else? Its soul could be wandering the Earth, or it could be in an afterlife, which raises the stakes and the difficulty of getting it back and getting them back together.

What if the body doesn't want that soul back, or what if this body is walking around and one of those spirits that's looking for a body is the one that takes over? As you can see, a lot of fun can be had with this kind of thinking. It is possible to create new undead types by combining different ideas that have already been done.

Unfinished Business

One of the frequently used ideas is that undead have unfinished business, and this is why they have stuck around.

Once again, this is nothing new, but you can use this idea when inventing something. What kind of unfinished business might keep someone here? If someone feels honor bound to complete a request that remained unfinished when they died, then this is one reason they might remain. One obligation could be looking after family members. The spirit might want to provide for them or protect them. In the *Star Wars* universe, sometimes dead Jedi look out for living Jedi. How many times do we hear Obi-Wan Kenobi say, "Use the force, Luke," to Luke Skywalker?

Now, when it comes to unfinished business, it's unlikely that two undead are going to have the exact same task that they want to complete. Why am I bringing this up? Well, because we're talking about inventing a type of undead. So, if two undead are unlikely to have the same goal, then it's unlikely that we can identify this undead type by the goal. Now, if the goal is regaining life by getting the body back, for example, that is something that can be common to an undead type. But, a specific goal for unfinished business, I think that's a little bit harder to imagine. What I mean is that the more specific that goal, the less likely it is that two people, or two undead, are going to share it. The general goal of unfinished business could be shared among an undead type, but the specific thing that each one of them wants to do is going to be different. This will likely be based on their personality and their life.

Torment

Another goal we might have for our undead type is to cause torment. If someone was a bully in life, or just obnoxious in general, then there's no reason to believe that they're going to change once they're dead, and then undead. In fact, their personal torment is probably significantly worse. And, therefore, their behavior might also be worse. The idea of tormenting people is kind of an old one. And, in more modern works, we've seen this idea of trying to understand undead types or monsters and just say, "Oh, well, they're not really evil. They just want something, and we're scared, and we've misunderstood."

And that's certainly a viable option, but there's no reason we can't go simple and just decide, yes, it's an evil spirit or an evil undead. It just wants to freak people out or scare them, even get them to kill themselves in some way, by accident or even just driving them to the point of committing suicide. If you have a number of undead types in your world, I would certainly make sure that one of them is simply evil. It's not misunderstood.

PEACE

On the other extreme is finding peace. Maybe this is what the undead really wants. And there are several versions of peace, one of those being a new life or going back to the afterlife, and then there is the option of simply being obliterated so that there is no afterlife for it at all and it is done, it's over. We might not think that this is a kind of peace, but, of course, there's no memory for this being once it's been completely destroyed. Here on Earth, we have this idea that the soul never really goes away. It just enters into a different state. And that's fine, but one of those states could be, yeah, that's it. It's done.

Since we already talked about regaining life, what about the option of regaining death? An undead might know that it wants this, but it might be unsure how to go about achieving it. In the case of a corporeal undead, it might assume that it can have its body be destroyed, and there-fore able to return to the afterlife. But, it may not actually be true. The body could just end up really decayed or something else, and the undead finds itself in an even worse situation than before.

Spiritual undead are often depicted as having no idea how to go about going to the afterlife, and that's one of the reasons why they are still here. They didn't do this on pur-pose. They're just stuck. These undead might be trying to find people who can help it. However, its ability to com-municate what it wants might be impaired, and we're going to talk about traits next. That includes communication.

UNDEAD TRAITS

It's time to talk about traits. These are what will define what our undead can and cannot do, and this is one of the best ways to distinguish one type from another. First up is speech and other sounds. In theory, a skeletal undead would have no ability to speak or make any sounds that don't involve its bones clacking together because, of course, it doesn't have a tongue. There are other parts of the body that are also missing, such as lungs and things in the throat that I'm not even going to name because I'm not someone that good with anatomy, but you know what I mean. All of that is gone.

However, as I mentioned in the last episode on undead, we assume that, if undead exist, that some supernatural agent is at work here, and that same agent could have given any of our undead the ability to speak. Even so, you may want to consider this when deciding if yours can. The ina-bility to communicate effectively, or at all, is one of the reasons why they can be frightening because we don't know what they want, and misunderstanding is one of the basic things that causes tension in a story. For that reason, having an undead speak perfectly is not something we typically see. A big exception to that has typically been vampires. But, remember that a vampire is usually only dead for just maybe a minute at most, so no decay has actually taken place. This is another reason to consider how long your undead must be dead before it can become undead.

Other types of corporeal undead have a decayed body, but it's not so far gone as a skeleton. And if they have decayed, then that could explain why the tongue is dried out and it's hard for them to communicate. This is a justification for something like moaning. We could always decide that our undead has telepathic abilities. However, once again, the ability to communicate so effectively might make them significantly less frightening. But, maybe that's what you want.

We could also have an undead produce a sound that has an effect on the living, and I don't mean just frightening them. I mean that maybe it causes us to go into a trance or be someone who is easily manipulated. Perhaps the sound draws us closer. Maybe it causes us to stop resisting.

Let's talk about touch. We briefly touched upon this in the last episode, but spirits are usually portrayed as being unable to touch anything in this world. However, sometimes we give them the ability to do so on rare occasions, such as being very upset. We could also decide they can only touch certain types of objects, or maybe they can only touch things at certain times of day, for example. Maybe it's only twilight and dusk. Maybe they can only touch certain types of people, like priests of a given religious order.

Something we've often seen is a spirit shown as being somehow weakened by this contact with the physical world. Giving someone a price is a good way to balance out the fact that they can glide right through walls, in this case.

In other words, if there's a pro to being in this undead state, then there's also a con. Whether it's a spiritual or corporeal undead, there's an idea that if they touch a person, that maybe something happens to the part of the body that is touched. For example, they could become infected, and maybe it has to be removed because nothing will stop this infection from spreading. Or maybe a magic spell or a technological item must be used to stop the spread. And what happens if that is not available? Well, possibly, this person turns into an undead. Or maybe they just turn into a monster of some kind. There's no reason undead have to create undead. They can always create a monster.

When it comes to spiritual undead, there's also the opposite problem. Can the living touch that spirit? Decide what impacts them. This is going to be relevant in a few minutes when we talk about how to destroy an undead.

Let's talk about movement. Spirits are often portrayed as having the ability to move right through a solid object. We can decide that they are doing this on purpose or that they don't recognize that the object is there. We could also decide that spirits don't have the ability to cross over certain types of materials, such as water or silver. There's a popular TV show called *Supernatural* where there's a kind of salt that they can spread on the ground and, therefore, nothing can pass over it. Then there's the most infamous idea, and that is that spirits or corporeal undead cannot go onto holy ground. Give some thought to whether your spirits or your corporeal undead are restricted in their movements. And once you create that restriction, decide how they can overcome that. You don't want them getting past it all the time, but you should use this as an option. It's always entertaining in a story when characters think they're safe because of some thing that's happened, and then it turns out they're not.

Another trait we should talk about is consumption. Does your undead type need to consume something to remain viable? Vampires are a good example of this. Besides blood, what else might something need to consume? We have a few options such as magical energy, consuming someone's soul or consuming some sort of energy that we would find in a science fiction story. The question then becomes how do they consume it? A skeleton has nothing to absorb something with if it tried to drink it. Another corporeal undead might have a mouth, but once it drinks something that's going to go into the stomach, it will probably leak out.

And, of course, spirits can't consume something that way at all. However, consuming does not necessarily mean drinking or eating, which is what we do when we're alive. Maybe they just need to expose themselves to something like radiation and absorb it. Give some thought whether your undead can consume anything, and how it does so. If you're looking for more ideas, there are more inside the *Creating Life* book.

Let's talk about their residence. After all, an undead has to be somewhere when it's not out and about terrorizing everybody. When it comes to spirits, we often don't consider this. I guess we assume that the spirit is in some sort of in-between place when it's not visible to those on Earth. After all, if it is returning to an afterlife and then coming back to the world, it's going to be doing this repeatedly. So, we might need some sort of explanation for that. Or we can just ignore the whole subject, which is what people seem to do typically. But if you're looking for one way to make your undead stand out, making a choice about this and making it interesting could be one way to do so.

You may want to invent another realm of existence, and this is where wandering spirits are when they are not on the world itself or in an afterlife. These alternate landscapes can often be useful, partly because we can send our characters into them in search of something or someone. I did this in my novella, *The Ever Fiend*, which you can download for free by joining my fantasy fiction newsletter.

When it comes to corporeal undead, they are either going to be wandering perpetually, even during daylight hours, or they're going to have to find somewhere to hide. This is essentially their residence, although it's certainly possible that they could be in a different place from night to night. One obvious place for them is a cemetery. But, of course, there's nothing new about that. Where else might they be found? Well, it's going to be anywhere where people don't typically go, and a ruined place is a good example of this. This could either be a place like a building or an entire city, or it could be an abandoned ship, for example.

Just like with monsters, you may want to decide where your undead is when it's not out terrorizing people, because this can really help you characterize it.

HOW CAN YOUR UNDEAD BE DESTROYED?

One of the subjects I'm not going to talk about today, but which is discussed in the book, *Creating Life*, is the appearance of your undead. This is a great way to make them different from other undead that we've already seen.

What I want to talk about next is death. Nothing lives forever, including undead. One of the things that your characters will most want to know about your undead type is how can they destroy it? For spirits, we often think that the final outcome is banishing them to some sort of afterlife. We tell ourselves that this is where they belong.

Something like a prison for a ghost would seem like a temporary measure instead of a final resolution.

A soul being destroyed utterly is another option. This oblivion is considered the worst possible outcome. After all, nothing is more final from this. You cannot come back from it. There is no chance at redemption or another life. If your manner of obliteration causes people to forget that you ever existed, that's even worse. Dead and forgotten forever is the worst possible fate, even though that's the one most of us will end up with. And that's probably one of the reasons we invented the idea of the afterlife.

Whether obliteration or being sent to an afterlife is the end result, how does our spirit end up getting there? We tend to assume that if it could do so on its own, it just would. Since it hasn't, it must be unable to. And, therefore, it needs help. Decide what form that help comes in. Is it a priest, or is it a magic spell or a technological item?

If the spirit was possessing a body, we should decide what happens to the person whose body has now been vacated. Have they gone insane? Have they recovered and they're just fine? Do they have no memory of what happened? Or, in the most interesting case, do they remember everything? And were they privy to knowledge that the other spirit had? They may have even experienced a kind of Stockholm Syndrome where they are in love with the spirit who has now been driven out. Are they now an ally of that spirit, and do they want to get it back or, in some way, help that person?

What about corporeal undead? How can they be destroyed? The most cliched answer is by fire, so we might want to do something different. Maybe this corporeal undead is, indeed, feeding on some sort of energy, and this energy can simply be drained from them. Maybe there's another kind of energy, whether it's technological or supernatural, that can have the opposite affect of, instead of giving them life, it gives them death. We tend to like this kind of symmetry.

There's a tendency to focus on destroying the body of a corporeal undead without much regard for what happens to the soul. Maybe we are all assuming that if you destroy that body, the soul then goes to its rightful afterlife. But does that really need to be the case? What if the soul just ends up becoming a spirit that's wandering and we've just traded one kind of undead for another? Regardless of your choice for how you destroy your undead, you must make one because this is one of the primary things your characters are going to wonder about.

WHERE TO START

Now I want to conclude today's episode by talking briefly about where to start with creating undead. Arguably, the first thing to do is consider whether there is an existing undead type that we can use instead of inventing one. It is almost certainly public domain. If you don't use it verbatim, you can still use it as the basis for your own undead by changing its basic appearance, behavior and imagining scenes of how this undead would frighten people or attack our characters.

I, personally, find it very helpful to imagine these scenes because it helps me figure out what I want to do, what I want to accomplish, and what I have already seen before and don't want to repeat myself. If you haven't already decided on whether it's a spiritual or corporeal undead, this is the time to do so. For ideas on what you can do, you can listen to this podcast episode, the previous one, or read the *Creating Life* book, the chapter on undead, which is chapter 7. And if you want, and you really want to get a head start on this, you can download the template on how to create undead from *The Art of World Building* website. You can start working on its fighting style and its behavior and abilities. And then, of course, there is deciding on how it can be killed.

Most of this can be invented in any order. My usual advice holds true. Do whatever you have an idea for first, and don't worry about getting it right. You can always review information on how to go about doing this and then come back to it later

ASSIGNING SENSES TO SPECIES

Hello and welcome to *The Art of World Building Podcast*, episode number twenty-two. Today's topic is about how to create your species' senses, from the five basics to other real senses humans and animals have, to sixth senses (second sight). Unlike previous episodes of this podcast, this material is not discussed in *The Art of World Building* book series.

THE FIVE SENSES

SIGHT

We'll start by talking about the five senses. The first up is going to be sight. Our default choice is to make the sight ordinary, just like us, or we can make their sight much better or worse than our own. So, for example, we could decide to have their eyes see much farther than we do, with clarity, or maybe we can decide that they can read really small print without any aid. We might also want to give them night vision if they are a species that's nocturnal, or if they're one that lives underground where there's not a lot of natural light. As I'm sure you're aware, night vision basically makes it seem as though it's much brighter, almost like there's a full moon. This could have a consequence, as well, where turning on the light is suddenly blinding to them, or maybe even daylight is that way naturally.

It's often a good idea to give a disadvantage when we're also giving them an advantage over us. That makes it seem like it balances out. We could also decide to give them infrared or heat vision that would let them see heat signatures. This is something that could also be useful at night or underground. Something like a forest-dwelling species, like elves in fantasy, might also find that helpful because there are so many things in the forest that it would be hard to see things unless some of them are giving off a heat signature that can be detected to help those items stand out for them. The ability of prey to hide behind underbrush would basically be eliminated.

We could also give them supernatural sight, like the ability to see spells that are active, and the ability to see spirits without any assistance. We could also give them the ability to see into other realms, or maybe just the openings into those realms. A normal person might need a spell, but this species can just detect these things automatically.

We might also want to give them the ability to detect energy fields, like different types of radiation, without having to use a technology to see this. This is obviously something that might be more useful in science fiction than fantasy. Then, of course, there's the infamous x-ray vision, like Superman, but I'm not sure that this is really practical or likely, and it could have a huge effect on that species' attitude about modesty and clothing. The concept of modesty might be completely lost on them.

Now, eyes that have any of these special features, we often want to give them a different look to them so that people can tell, just by looking at the species, that their eyes are different and have another capability. This is especially useful in a visual medium like TV and film. One way to do that is to give an unusual pigment to the iris or to create different shaped pupils.

I've listed a lot of things we can do with eyes, but you certainly don't want to do all of these. That would be overkill. You probably only want to give one special ability to a given species. In fact, in an entire setting, you might only want to have one species with unusual sight capabilities.

HEARING

Let's talk a little bit about hearing. Once again, we can make this ordinary, just like humans, or we can give them the ability to hear much fainter sounds, or even have them be bothered by sounds that we would consider to be not that loud, but to them it's deafening. We can also give them the ability to hear sounds that are farther away than something that we would hear. We could also increase their frequency range so that they can hear sounds that are lower or higher that we would not even notice. They might also have the ability to tell which direction a sound is coming from in conditions where this is not so easy, such as a big hall where there's a lot of reverberation. Sometimes, in the wilderness, it might be hard to tell which direction a sound really came from. We might have a general sense, but maybe this species has a much more specific sense.

Another issue that we can have in a place that's pretty noisy is that sometimes we can't isolate a sound, such as the person that's talking directly to us. We might be hearing too much noise from other people and we just can't focus on that person that we want to hear. So, maybe this species is better at that. This is more likely of a species that spends a lot of time in such a place, such as, maybe, dwarves because anywhere underground is probably going to have a lot of echoes to it.

Now, this one isn't particularly exciting, and it may not even be that useful to us, so we should try to figure out what might benefit our story when we're trying to think of any of the senses that I talk about in this episode. Maybe their ability to pick up a new language is improved because they have a better ability to pick apart the separate sounds into syllables and words. That's another skill, and a very useful one. Maybe they can even understand what animals are trying to communicate to us with the way they make various sounds. And, of course, they could have supernatural talents, like the ability to hear spirits, voices or even other people's thoughts. That last one seems to be more of a mental trait than an actual hearing trait, but it's still something we can consider.

FEEL

When it comes to their sense of feel, once again, is this better or worse than humans? Maybe they're supersensitive or hyperaware of certain sensations, or the opposite. And they may have a higher or lower pain threshold, which could certainly be useful in battle. Most of us probably think it would be great to not be able to feel pain, but I remember seeing a story a long time ago about a little girl who could not feel pain. As a result, she made herself go blind. Why did that happen? Well, because she kept sticking her finger up to her eye and scratching her eyeball with her finger. She was too young to understand not to do that and she did it so many times that she literally made herself go blind. There were other issues, too, such as hurting our self, but not feeling it. So, therefore, she didn't know and her parents had to constantly check her for injuries because she would never tell them because she was totally unaware of it. Anything going on with an internal organ might also be a problem because that usually causes pain if there's a problem. But if you don't feel that and nobody can see it, you're going to have no idea.

Another sense that we could give them is the ability to feel changes in atmosphere and pressure. As a result, maybe they would be able to tell that a storm is coming. They might also be able to sense vibrations. That could possibly work as an early detection of earthquakes. They could also possibly sense temperature changes more quickly, or be immune to them. I can tell you that, as someone who rides a motorcycle, when I go through a cool spot at 60 miles an hour, I definitely feel that. So, even a flying species, if it's moving that fast, would probably be able to feel that more than I would if they've got a super sense for it.

Another thing we can do is have different parts of their body be more sensitive to either pain or pleasure. If memory serves me right, the Ferengi from *Star Trek* have these really large ears and they enjoy having those be stroked. We can do something similar.

TASTE

When it comes to our sense of taste, this is a hard one to make useful in a story because, unless our characters are eating or drinking something, or they're going around licking a lot of things, we're not going to have much use for this. However, we could decide that their tongues are more or less sensitive to various kinds of tastes, or that those tastes last longer or shorter for them. We could also reverse their tastes so that foods taste differently to them. Maybe something that's sweet to us is sour for them, and vice versa. I think the only use we might have for such a thing is for someone to exhibit disgust at a meal, and inadvertently offend the host.

Something that might be more interesting is the ability to tell what ingredients went into something that they are either eating or drinking, with some level of accuracy. This could be especially important if something like a poison has been used. Maybe there's even a potion and they can basically reverse engineer the ingredients of that potion by drinking just a little bit, or just tasting it. Obviously, with a poison, you wouldn't want to ingest a lot of it, but, of course, a lot of poisons, you need to consume a certain amount for it to have an effect on you.

SMELL

The last of the normal senses we'll talk about is smell. We can, once again, make this just like us, or better and worse than us. Maybe a smell lingers longer, or they can smell something that is fainter that basically originated farther in the past. Then there's the idea of the bloodhound being able to follow a scent for a long time. Maybe they can smell something that we might not notice, and this is important. For example, we can smell smoke and realize that there's a fire. Maybe they can smell something else and realize there's a different kind of danger present. Maybe they can, once again, reverse engineer a scent from a food or drink and interpret the ingredients. They might even be able to tell how many people have left a scent in a room and, from that, they could tell how many people were present at a meeting. If they know the scent of those people, maybe they can tell who was present. They might also be able to tell which direction each person left from that room.

So, that concludes our talk about the basic senses. After this, we're going to talk about some other ones you may not have ever heard of.

OTHER SENSES

ELECTROCEPTION

So, we've all heard of the five senses, which were made famous by Aristotle a long time ago. But, as it turns out, modern scientists actually think we have a whole bunch more of them. The first one we're going to look at is electroception. This is the ability to sense electrical fields. On Earth, this is almost exclusively aquatic life. They're the ones who can do this. If you watched enough nature shows about ocean life, you've probably run across this. Now, the reason it's only in the water for the most part is that water conducts electricity much better than air or solids, which you're probably aware of.

With this sense comes the ability to do electrolocation. In other words, this is finding objects in either the dark or in muddy water. This is almost like sonar in the sense that different types of objects reflect back electricity, or a lack thereof. So, for example, a rock is not going to show anything, but a fish will. So, if you've got a fish that has this electroception, it is going to be able to tell that there is a living thing there, versus something that's not alive. Another way that this is used is to avoid predators by sensing that they are near and stopping their own motion so that they don't give off their location.

There are two types of electroception. One of them is called active. Basically, that means that the animal can generate a small electric field that isn't much bigger than they are. For example, if you've got a fish that's two inches long, then maybe this field extends two inches from them in every direction. The other is passive, and that's just the ability to sense electrical fields. All living organisms give off that energy. So, if I hold very still in the water, an animal that has this passive electroception would be able to tell that I'm there, even if I'm not moving.

Something else we can do with this is electrocommunication. Basically, what these animals do is they change the wavelength that is generated and use that as a way to signal other animals, which can be for mating or for a territorial display to make themselves seem like they're more intimidating to scare away a dangerous animal, such as the electric eel. As a side note, the electric eel is able to generate a much stronger pulse, which is used to stun animals, but it's not enough to hurt us. However, we can always give that ability to a water-dwelling species of ours so that they can hurt, and maybe even kill is. For the most part, if you're going to use electroception, you probably want to use it for a water-dwelling species and not try to give it to something that's on land.

NOCICEPTION

Then there's nociception, which is the ability to detect pain. I alluded to this earlier. There are basically three major categories of pain. One is mechanical, which is something like cutting or crushing pain. Then there's thermal, which is heat or cold. And then there's chemical, which is any kind of toxin. This is a sense that we definitely have. We have it most strongly in our skin, followed by our joints and then in our internal organs. And we have responses to pain, which can include a pallor or sweating, nausea and, in more extreme cases, fainting. A way we can use this with our invented species is to change the reaction or the degree of these. We're basically looking to make them different from us in some way.

TIME SENSES

Then there's our sense of time, which we have. But things can go wrong with this. In science fiction, with space travel, we can definitely leverage this. Our time sense has to do with estimating time intervals, and the duration of them, and whether events are simultaneous or not. There are some temporal illusions, and one of them is called telescoping. This is when we recall that events happened farther in the past than they really did. Another problem we can have is that sometimes we overestimate how short an interval is, or the opposite of that, underestimating how long an interval was. The most practical example of this that I've seen in films is when a witness to a crime is having trouble remembering how much time really passed.

Another interesting temporal illusion is that if a lot of things happen in a short period, we can perceive that as there being more time passing. But if almost nothing happened in a short period of time, we will overestimate how much time has passed. It goes back to that expression: "Time flies when you're having fun." Well, if you're having a lot of fun, you can think that much more time has passed than has actually occurred. On the other hand, if you're really bored, time can seem like it's really dragging out.

You're probably familiar with SF and space travel and the concept of time dilation. This means that two observers think that a different amount of time has passed due to them being different distances to a gravitational field, or their velocities relative to each other are quite different. Faster than light travel does not cause time dilation. Now, this is fictional, so that's really just a theory, but we've got jump drive, warp drive and hyperdrive – which I talked about in a previous episode – and none of those cause this. On the other hand, slower than light travel is real and, if the velocities are high enough, this can cause time dilation. But we could decide that the species we are inventing is basically immune to this effect. Maybe they've even programmed their devices to counteract it as well.

MAGNETOCEPTION

Another interesting and real-life sense is magnetoception. This is the ability to detect a magnetic field. This can be used for direction sense, altitude or location. This is one that we can not only give our species, but any of the animals that we invent. On that note, animals use this sense to mentally map a region. This is also why an animal can migrate really long distances without using landmarks, or even doing this in the dark so they don't need to see where they're going. Since humans don't have that sense, or it's very weak, we tend to use things like the position of the sun, or the moss growing on the north side of the tree in the northern hemisphere, or the opposite in the southern hemisphere, or an actual device like a compass. You could certainly give a strong magnetoception to one of your species so that they are like a living compass. Imagine how valued they would be by any traveling companions because they're probably not going to get lost very often.

MAGICEPTION

The last sense I want to talk about is a fictional one. I'm just going to make up the name "magiception," or, in other words, the ability to sense magical energy. This could definitely be useful in a world with magic. If you've got this sense, maybe you can tell what spell has been cast or how long ago it was cast. Maybe you can tell whether that spell is strong or weak, and whether it's fading in strength. You may even be able to tell what type of magic it is if there is more than one type of magic in your setting. You may even have the ability to sense an anti-magic zone; somewhere where magic is not capable of being performed. You probably want to decide how far from the body this sense extends. Is it only a few inches, maybe a body length or even more than that? And how does their body react when they sense something here?

This is a possible trait for a species that is from a highly magical habitat because this would probably come in handy. Or maybe they're a highly magical species that has been highly magical for thousands of years and, as a result, this sense of theirs has increased. Or they could be a species that has routinely been victimized by magic for thousands of years, whether that's from their habitat or from others doing things to them.

My last note on some of these is that you generally only want to assign one unusual trait to one of your species because if you start giving them too many, it just starts to seem a little bit weird. We might also want to decrease one sense when we are augmenting another, again, for that sense of balance and fairness. We don't want them to become overly powerful. And we may want to try to find a reason that they have that trait, such as it being caused by their original habitat.

THE SIXTH SENSE

TELEPATHY

It's time to talk about second sight, which is also called a sixth sense. These include clairvoyance, telepathy, psychometry, precognition and mediumship.

Telepathy is the ability to communicate with the minds of others through thought instead of having to talk, use body language or anything like that. Despite what some might think, this is a fictional ability. It is often used in science fiction and fantasy, so you are probably familiar with seeing this depicted.

Before giving one of our species this ability, we may want to consider their habitat and their culture before deciding on it. Both their speech and their hearing being compromised might lead them to need an alternate form of communication. So, as I talked about earlier, when we give someone an augmented ability, like telepathy, we might want to reduce something else like, in this case, either their hearing or their speech to make them weaker in that area. This could make it naturally harder for them to communicate with other species who are not telepaths.

So, if they are pretty isolated, they stick to themselves, and they're all telepaths, then when they interact with others, they're going to have some issues. We don't have to do that, but it's one way to balance them out. I think if they can still speak and hear fine, then this implies that they still interact with other species quite regularly, or that they've only somewhat recently become telepaths and they don't rely on this exclusively. The opposite is also implied. If they have suffered an impaired speech or hearing ability, that would suggest that they really are isolated and they've been telepaths for a long time.

A noisy environment might also put them in a position where they develop telepathy because it's just easier to communicate that way. Another potential issue is that maybe predators use this for soundless communication so that it's easy for them to sneak up on their prey, but they can still communicate with each other. We might want to decide if everyone in the species can do it or if it's just certain individuals, and why that might be. Maybe people need to reach a certain age or have a certain experience, such as maybe the first menstruation for a woman, or maybe losing your virginity for either gender.

We should also decide if people can control who hears them, or are they an open book and pretty much anyone can hear them, the same way that if you were shouting in a loud room, everyone who's present is going to hear what you're saying. And then how far do they have to be from another person in order to do this? Is there a distance requirement? Can they not be more than 10 feet apart? Maybe they have to be touching each other. These are ways to give them limitations on this ability so that they're not all-powerful and god-like.

CLAIRVOYANCE

Clairvoyance is another second sight that we can give our species. This is the ability to witness future or past people, locations, events or objects. And no contact or association with that is needed. They can do it regardless of having never met those people, been in that location or touched that object, for example. However, if we are looking for a limit, we can change that and decide they have to have some sort of association. Distance is also usually not considered a factor with clairvoyants, but we can also add that as a limitation. And I do think that between worlds, this would be a reasonable limitation. But, on the other hand, we might want to have someone who is so incredibly powerful as a clairvoyant that they can even do this across worlds. This is something that's probably going to come up more in science fiction than fantasy.

In one of the recent *Star Wars* movies, Luke Skywalker basically projects himself from across, maybe, the whole galaxy, but this act is basically his final act because it essentially kills him. Or, at least, it appears to have killed him. We won't really know until the next film comes out. This is a pretty severe limit to put on someone, and we could decide, instead, that it just weakens them. Although, of course, in the case of Luke Skywalker, he was doing that across such vast distances that it makes sense that this would be an even more serious toll. But we might want to decide that there are things that need to happen before someone can do this, such as maybe a ritual, or maybe they have to do it at a certain time of the day or month, or maybe the stars have to be aligned a certain way. Maybe they need to be submerged in some sort of special liquid, earth or even a gas, or possibly use drugs in order to enhance the ability to do this.

Now, there are some limitations that seem to be baked into clairvoyance, and one of them is that they cannot control how much they see when they are doing this far sight. They also can't control how long they see an event. So, they might not see the entire thing from beginning to end. They might only see, maybe, the middle of this. Therefore, this is open to interpretation, so what they learn is compromised and they have to figure out the context of this without really having that. Maybe this leads to misunderstanding. So, that is definitely something that could happen to any of us if we were only seeing part of a story.

If we're trying to decide what species should have the ability to be a clairvoyant, then one that doesn't travel much is a good option because maybe they use this as a way to learn about the larger world that they seldom visit. So, a species that lives underground is a good choice, and so is one that is underwater.

PSYCHOMETRY

Another sixth sense we can talk about is psychometry. This is the ability to learn information about an object upon contact with it. These objects are thought to have some sort of energy field that can be sensed. The things that can be learned are, maybe, who owns that object or who last touched it. We can also decide that they can tell how it came to be where it is. Maybe they know its origins or what its future demise is going to be. We might also decide that they can sense the role that this has had in past events, present events or maybe even future events if any of these are going to be significant. As with all of these senses, we might want to limit just how many of those options I listed they can actually do, and how accurate their sense really is.

Then there's the question of how things are learned when they touch it. Do they see images? Maybe they hear sounds. Do they just get vague impressions or can they sense the emotions that are around this object? We can decide that any or all of these are present, but they could also just be fleeting images or sounds that can be very jumbled so that it's very hard to understand, or we can decide that it's kind of like a perfect audio and video feed of a clip somewhere and we have perfect sight into what exactly is going on. Now, if we do that, I would recommend making it a very short amount of stuff that they can see. Otherwise, again, they just become extremely powerful.

When thinking of limitations, you really want to think of how this can impact your story if this person doesn't get it right. What if they have some misinformation and the characters act on that and then that causes a problem? In general, that's something you want to do to some degree or another because, otherwise, it's just too easy for everyone.

PRECOGNITION

Let's talk about precognition. This is the ability to see events before they occur. Seeing an event after it has occurred is called retrocognition. We should once again place limits on the ability to interpret these events. One of the reasons for this is that the events may not occur that way after all, partly due to misunderstanding and the future not being set because, of course, we do have free choice and free will, and things may not turn out as someone thinks they will.

The last question to ask about this, again, is who might have this skill. A species that is likely to cause significant future changes might have some ability to predict how those are going to turn out. On the other hand, a species that is going to be especially affected by such changes might also have the ability. Maybe the future is putting out some sort of energy, like Armageddon is approaching, and this could result in the birth of a precog to warn people to prevent this calamity from happening. It's almost like the Earth itself is going to give some sort of warning through the precog, and this person can then go on to warn people, and this disaster be averted.

MEDIUMSHIP

The last one I want to talk about is mediumship. This is the ability to see, hear and/or feel spirits with or without spells, rituals, drugs or devices. It basically means communication with the dead. There are different variants on how this can happen, but in this case we're really just focusing on whether a species can do it. I will leave it up to you to decide on how they go about doing so. As with many of these second sights, if your species has the ability to do this, they are probably going to be somewhat known for this. So, decide if that's something you want.

So, what species might have the ability to do mediumship? Well, if your species does not have a written language, or it's only got a protolanguage like pictograms or ideograms, and it's not an alphabet or a logography, that means that they cannot pass down details about the past to those who are still living. Therefore, if we want to learn about the past, maybe we use mediums to contact people who were still alive back then and who are now dead.

Another justification for a species having a mediumship capability is that they might have a complex afterlife, which is difficult to navigate and get to where they're supposed to be. Somewhere like heaven. So, we might need to be able to communicate with the spirits of the recently deceased to guide them to their final resting place.

And, as with everything, you're going to want to place some limitations on the ability to do this, such as requiring rituals, an artifact from the dead or just anything to make it not so easy to do this and just contact anybody. You're going to have to place a limit so that they can only reach certain people and they can't get complete information. That just makes it too easy for them, and that means there's no drama in our story

Appendix

This appendix includes sections repeated in most episodes.

Review

If you're enjoying the podcast, please rate and review the show at artofworldbuilding.com/review. Reviews really are critical to encouraging more people to listen to a show haven't heard of before, and it can also help the show rank better, allowing more people to discover it. Again that URL is artofworldbuilding.com/review.

Subscribe

So, let's talk about how to subscribe to this podcast. A podcast is a free, downloadable audio show that enables you to learn while you're on the go. To subscribe to my podcast for free, you'll need an app to listen to the show from.

For iPhone, iPad, and iPod listeners, grab your phone or device and go to the iTunes Store and search for *The Art of World Building.* This will help you to download the free podcast app, which is produced by Apple, and then subscribe to the show from within that app. Every time I produce a new episode, you'll get it downloaded right onto your device.

For Android listeners, you can download the Stitcher radio app, and search for *The Art of World Building.*

This only needs to be done once and at that point, you will never miss an episode.

MORE RESOURCES

Let's take a quick break here and talk about where you can get more useful world building resources. Artofworldbuilding.com has most of what you need. This includes links to more podcasts like this one. You can also find more information on all three volumes of *The Art of World Building* series. Much of the content of those books is available on the website for free.

And the thing that you might find most useful is that by signing up for the newsletter, you can download the free templates that are included with each volume of *The Art of World Building* series, whether you have bought the books or not. All you need to do is join the newsletter. You can do this by going to artofworldbuilding.com/newsletter. Sign up today and you will get your free templates, and you will never miss an update about what is happening in the great world of world building.

More books are available in the series, including two workbooks, all at Amazon: https://amzn.to/3y7mN1B

PATREON SUPPORT

For those of you who support crowdfunding, I am on the patreon site and would appreciate any support you can lend. Think about whether you're benefiting from this podcast or The Art of World Building blog and website, and consider supporting the effort to spread the word far and wide. Your support could help a budding world builder create an awesome world that you become a huge fan of. This podcast and related items are my way of giving back to the fantasy, sci-fi, movie, and gaming industries that I love so much. You can give back too by helping to fund this effort. When the next Tolkien or George R.R. Martin shows up, you can tell yourself, "I helped him do that!"

Your support can be just $1 a month to the cause. Higher levels of support get you increasingly cool things, such as PDF transcripts of this podcast, free mp3s (including unreleased music), free eBooks and short stories, bookmarks, and even signed copies of books and CDs of my music. Many of these are unavailable to the public.

Just go to artofworldbuilding.com/patreon. You can also just go to the home page and click the big icon for this. Support great world building today!

WORLD BUILDING UNIVERSITY

If you'd like to learn world building skills through instruction, I've launched World Building University. There you can find one free course you can take just by signing up, which has no obligation. Other courses are in development and available now. You can preview parts of every course, all of which include video lessons, quizzes, assignments, and sometimes downloadable templates that are even better than those found in the books.

To get your first free course, just go to worldbuilding.university.

Closing

All of this show's music is actually courtesy of yours truly, as I'm also a musician. The theme song is the title track from my *Some Things Are Better Left Unsaid* album. You can hear more songs at RandyEllefson.com. Check out artofworldbuilding.com for free templates to help with your world building. And please rate and review the show in iTunes. Thanks for listening

About The Author

Randy Ellefson has written fantasy fiction for decades and is an avid world builder, having spent three decades creating Llurien. He has a Bachelor of Music in classical guitar but has always been more of a rocker, having released several albums and earned endorsements from music companies. He's an IT professional in the Washington D.C. suburbs. He loves spending time with his son and daughter when not writing, making music, or playing golf.

Connect with me online:

http://www.RandyEllefson.com
http://twitter.com/RandyEllefson
http://facebook.com/RandyEllefsonAuthor

If you like this book, please help others enjoy it.

Lend it. Please share this book with others.
Recommend it. Please recommend it to friends, family, reader groups, and discussion boards
Review it. Please review the book at Goodreads and the vendor where you bought it.

JOIN THE RANDY ELLEFSON NEWSLETTER!

Subscribers receive a FREE book, discounts, exclusive bonus scenes, and the latest updates!

www.ficiton.randyellefson.com/newsletter

Randy Ellefson Books

Talon Stormbringer

Talon is a sword-wielding adventurer who has been a thief, pirate, knight, king, and more in his far-ranging life.

The Ever Fiend
The Screaming Moragul

www.fiction.randyellefson.com/talonstormbringer

The Dragon Gate Series

Four unqualified Earth friends are magically summoned to complete quests on other worlds, unless they break the cycle – or die trying.

Volume 1: *The Dragon Gate*
Volume 2: *The Light Bringer*
Volume 3: *The Silver-Tongued Rogue*
Volume 4: *The Dragon Slayer*
Volume 5: *The Majestic Magus*

www.fiction.randyellefson.com/dragon-gate-series/

The Ascension Quest Series

When Max awakens in the VRMMORPG game Llurien Online, he doesn't know how he got there or why he can't logout. And a Life Counter no other player has is steadily descending to zero. Can he escape before he dies?

Death Singer

www.fiction.randyellefson.com/ascension-quest-litrpg-series

THE ART OF WORLD BUILDING

This is a multi-volume guide for authors, screenwriters, gamers, and hobbyists to build more immersive, believable worlds fans will love.

Volume 1: *Creating Life*
Volume 2: *Creating Places*
Volume 3: *Cultures and Beyond*
Volume 4: *Creating Life: The Podcast Transcripts*
Volume 5: *Creating Places: The Podcast Transcripts*
Volume 6: *Cultures and Beyond: The Podcast Transcripts*
185 Tips on World Building
3000 World Building Prompts
The Complete Art of World Building
The Art of the World Building Workbook: Fantasy Edition
The Art of the World Building Workbook: Sci-Fi Edition

Visit www.artofworldbuilding.com for details.

Randy Ellefson Music

Instrumental Guitar

Randy has released three albums of hard rock/metal instrumentals, one classical guitar album, and an all-acoustic album. Visit http://www.music.randyellefson.com for more information, streaming media, videos, and free mp3s.

2004: The Firebard
2007: Some Things Are Better Left Unsaid
2010: Serenade of Strings
2010: The Lost Art
2013: Now Weaponized!
2014: The Firebard (re-release)

www.ingramcontent.com/pod-product-compliance
Lightning Source LLC
Chambersburg PA
CBHW031120020426
42333CB00012B/165